PRAISE FOR

HALF BROKE

"Fascinating. . . . Some of the most compelling characters here don't speak in words: They are horses. And in [Ginger] Gaffney's story, they come alive." —Deborah Hopkinson, *BookPage*

"With sensitive, soul-baring prose, Ginger Gaffney weaves together her personal experiences as a horse trainer with the struggles of damaged humans and damaged horses. I was also moved by the depth of vulnerability and intuition of the horses. As Lorin Lindner's *Birds of a Feather* reveals for traumatized parrots and soldiers, so *Half Broke* reveals for horses and parolees." —Jonathan Balcombe, author of *What a Fish Knows*

"Ginger Gaffney is a bold and original talent. . . . Savor this book, and then buy a copy for your best friend." —Anne Hillerman, *New York Times* best-selling author

"Gaffney pulls off the impressive feat of translating horses and humans. She creates lyricism through experience, landscape, and empathy." —Gretchen Lida, *Washington Independent Review of Books*

"This marvelous memoir, peopled with folks in serious trouble of one kind or another, and the horses they care for, creatures with their own sophisticated ways of communicating, taught me as much about language as have my seventy-seven years on the planet." —Abigail Thomas, author of *What Comes Next and How to Like It*

HALF BROKE

HALF BROKE

a memoir

GINGER GAFFNEY

W. W. NORTON & COMPANY
Independent Publishers Since 1923

For information about permission to reproduce selections from this book, write to
Permissions, W. W. Norton & Company, Inc., 500 Fifth Avenue, New York, NY 10110

For information about special discounts for bulk purchases, please contact
W. W. Norton Special Sales at specialsales@wwnorton.com or 800-233-4830

Manufacturing by LSC Communications
Book design by Chris Welch
Production manager: Lauren Abbate

Library of Congress Cataloging-in-Publication Data

Names: Gaffney, Ginger, author.
Title: Half broke : a memoir / Ginger Gaffney.
Description: First edition. | New York, NY : W. W. Norton & Company, [2020]
Identifiers: LCCN 2019030052 | ISBN 9781324003076 (hardcover) |
ISBN 9781324003083 (epub)
Subjects: LCSH: Gaffney, Ginger. | Horse trainers—United States—Biography. | Horses—
Training—New Mexico. | Horses—Therapeutic use—New Mexico. | Criminals—
Rehabilitation—New Mexico. | Human-animal relationships.
Classification: LCC SF284.52.G34 A3 2020 | DDC 798.2092 [B]—dc23
LC record available at https://lccn.loc.gov/2019030052

ISBN 978-0-393-54154-0 pbk.

W. W. Norton & Company, Inc., 500 Fifth Avenue, New York, N.Y. 10110
www.wwnorton.com

W. W. Norton & Company Ltd., 15 Carlisle Street, London W1D 3BS

1 2 3 4 5 6 7 8 9 0

For Glenda

"All of us go onto the ranch—spiritually, mentally, emotionally, physically, and financially—broken. But we each have a sliver of hope. The aliveness within us has a soft voice. Otherwise, none of us would have come here in the first place."

—*Eliza*

CONTENTS

AUTHOR'S NOTE

This book represents my best recollection of the events I relate. During the year and a half these events took place, I worked with over fifty residents. Some characters are composites. The dialogue comes from memory and from conversations I had with residents after they left the ranch. These conversations often led to differing accounts of the same events which I have tried to integrate.

HALF BROKE

PROLOGUE

At first it seemed like just another ranch asking me to help. Training horses and educating their owners has been my job for the last twenty years. I hear many stories of horse trouble. In those stories a lot of things go unsaid and, most likely, unnoticed. But I know that the slightest movement—a flick of an ear, a shortening of breath—is how a horse will try to communicate. If the owners had noticed this subtle language early on, the whole bad experience might have gone differently. But this call was different. Not once in my life had I heard of horses acting like this: scavenging, marauding, war parties of horses. I didn't think it could be true, and if it was, I certainly needed to see it.

This particular ranch is a prison. Most of the residents living here are multiple offenders, felons. They applied to come to the ranch from prison and have gone before a judge to have the term of their sentence finished here on the ranch. The whole operation is run by the residents themselves: no hired CEO, no lawyers, no counselors, no outside plumbers, no doctors. No jail guards. Statewide and county judges, probation and parole officers, court-appointed lawyers—all interact and count on the older residents of this ranch to fulfill the legal sentencing requirements for each resident.

This ranch has run like this for almost fifty years. The oldest residents take the lead and teach each new arrival the essential skills to keep the operation of the ranch ongoing. Only a few of the residents have come in off the streets voluntarily, strung out on heroin, meth, or alcohol. They live at the ranch after hitting rock bottom. This ranch is here to save their lives.

Horses have always been part of the ranch. They live together with the residents on this seventeen-acre property, which sits along the banks of the Rio Grande in northern New Mexico. The herd roams free in the pastures. They gather in the automotive shop when it rains and snows, and in the woodshop when the flies get too bad. They forage through the ranch dumpsters for cookies, leftover baked goods, and Wonder Bread. At night they are chased by six to eight men, running behind them, into sizeable pens where they have shelter, water, and alfalfa hay. During the day they wander the property like giant gods with dominion over all things.

No one on the ranch knows very much about horses. They don't know that Wonder Bread and Tastykakes are not good forage for an animal that has browsed on grasses, flowers, and tree bark for thousands of years. Before I got the call, the horses had begun running in packs like dogs, chasing the residents when they brought the trash out from the cafeteria after breakfast, lunch, and dinner. The residents gathered in a tight circle next to the trash containers. They carved wooden poles in their woodshop that they carried to fend off each attack. Residents had been bitten, they'd been tripped and stepped on. A few had injuries to their ankles, arms, and wrists. Men and women, toughened by prison and living on the streets, ran as fast as they could for safety when the horses began their charge.

My first trip to the ranch was on a Sunday. Sunday is the one day of the week the residents have off from a grueling weekly work schedule. At the ranch, they have a livestock division. The residents working on livestock are required to feed and care for the horses, ducks, dogs, and cats that live on the property. There are two heads of the livestock division and about six other members who split duties of caring for the animals.

I learned on that first Sunday that the livestock division was run by two women, Flor and Sarah. Flor was in her thirties, a longtime heroin addict for fifteen years. She was in prison for a multitude of crimes, with the last term for robbing her mother's home. Her mother turned her in, feeling certain that prison was the safest place for Flor. Flor is a small woman with a big presence. When I first met her, she stood with her legs parted wide, her chest and shoulders open, arms draped by her side, as she looked me straight in the eye. Sarah was in her forties, a mother, a meth and heroin addict, and a prostitute since she was thirteen. When she spoke to me, her body wiggled like she was dancing. Her mouth held wrinkles that pointed the corners of her lips toward the ground.

Everything at the ranch, all the knowledge and skill it takes to keep the property in good order and the residents cared for and well fed, is supervised by the residents who have lived here the longest. The elder residents are the officials in charge. It is a long chain of knowledge handed down, one person at a time, ensuring that the strong traditions and standards of the ranch will continue. At one time there had been a chain of knowledge regarding how to care for the horses. That chain of knowledge had broken. Neither Flor nor Sarah had much experience with horses, yet they understood something was seriously wrong.

They went before the elders of the ranch and asked permission to reach into the community for help. Asking for and receiving help from outside the ranch is rarely needed. Most of the residents come from families with a long history of addiction, poverty, and gang crime. Some of them have never worked a job in their entire life. *Each one, teach one*—this is the way the ranch operates. Every four months the residents change jobs to learn a new skill: plumbing, cooking, auto mechanics. The older residents pass on their knowledge. Over one hundred residents live on the ranch at any one time. Drug addicts and criminals adjusting to life outside a conventional prison but still contained by twelve-foot adobe walls.

That's when I got the call. I am a small-framed woman, weighing just over 120 pounds. I can be quiet and reserved when I first meet people and rarely make dramatic first impressions. My calm, restrained demeanor may not impress people, but horses take to it easily. In my work over the past twenty years, I have witnessed a wide variation of behavior when it comes to the horse-human relationship. On that first Sunday, I found myself in the middle of the most dangerous horse situation I had ever encountered.

EMOTIONAL
CAMOUFLAGE

March / 2013

The men and women from the livestock team are sitting on tables and benches placed under the shelter of a small tack room, positioned a few yards away from the nighttime corrals. It is four in the afternoon, feeding time. Recently they have experienced bad accidents during the feeding routine. Arguments about whose fault it was and the question of how to fix the problems are on their minds. I introduce myself to everyone, as each member of the team rises to shake my hand and tell me their name. They begin to talk. The most recent accident, with Paul, keeps coming up. Paul was trampled by Hawk two days ago. His left wrist is wrapped in a support bandage, and he limps along dragging his right leg.

"How can we keep them from running us over? I mean, they

don't listen," Paul explains. Paul is a tall man, with a thick neck and broad shoulders. "They run right through us, like we aren't even here," he tells me. His ear lobes have wide open holes at their end. I see straight through them like I'm looking through tiny windows.

"And this is always at dinnertime, or other times, too?" I ask.

"Always at dinner and anytime there's food."

A tall, thin man rises off the bench to shake my hand. His name is Rex. He grins as he unbuttons his collared shirt to show me a perfect hoof-shaped bruise on his chest.

"Scout knocked me good yesterday during the morning feed," he tells me as he gestures out into the pasture to a brown-and-white spotted horse standing away from the rest of the herd. "I was dropping the hay into his trough when he spun around and got me." Rex is taller than Paul, six-foot-three at least. Lean and lanky, he towers over me with his shirt unbuttoned, looking down at me with his hazel green eyes.

I hesitate. "I want to see how it goes," I tell the group. "Let's bring them in and feed."

A young man named Marcus rises from the bench. He has the body of a guy who spends too much time in the gym. His muscles bulge under his tight T-shirt and make his upper torso move like a large stone. He looks a little angry, yet he speaks carefully. I wonder if my presence makes him nervous. I get the feeling that not everyone on livestock is happy to have my help.

"Let's get 'em, guys."

The other men rise off the bench at his command. Marcus walks over, unlatches the hay barn door, swings it open, and starts throwing small portions of alfalfa hay into the arms of the waiting men. The horses stand at the far end of the pasture, heads down and quietly chewing. With the sound of the latch and the barn door swinging open, they snap their heads from the ground, readying themselves to race in our direction. Each man grabs two cuts of alfalfa, tucks them tight against his body, and launches into a run toward the night corrals. They toss the hay into the feed troughs and tear back to the shelter of the tack-room shed, intent and out of breath. A few of the men make a second trip back to the corrals to ensure that each horse has enough hay for the night. Flor, Sarah, and the others cram themselves into the front of the hay barn, shouting like they are participating in an important sporting event.

"Hurry up. Here they come. Get in here!"

The residents' screaming paralyzes me. And then, here they come—the horses galloping, ears back, kicking up and thundering toward us. I am standing alongside the large cottonwood tree that shades the barn and night corrals. A herd of horses racing across a field has a mesmerizing effect. Most of my days are filled with teaching horses how to feel comfortable in the world of humans. But my secret truth is that I love their world more. All they need is their bodies. As they gallop toward us I see their legs churn under the wide girths of their rib cages.

The shouting and screaming grows louder, and a few of the men run out and grab me, dragging me back inside the hay barn. Marcus slams the gate behind us. We are all tucked into an eight-foot-wide space in front of the hay. The horses roar up to the wooden gate at a gallop, a band of snaked bodies, twisting and kicking dirt into the air. They level their heads and necks down to the height of their shoulders, flat and thin, ready to strike.

It sounds like a hiss, but it's more like spit. Hawk opens his mouth and his teeth jut forward at us. He snaps his jaw shut and curls back his lips. The force of it shoots a mist of saliva all over our faces. He can see us—they all can—but they cannot get to us. Their dark hollow eyes are unrecognizable to me. Watching them bare their teeth at us like predators, as if we were their meal, makes me think: these are not horses.

We are their captives, herded into our cell like lesser animals. They stand in front of the gate swinging their necks back and forth, ears flat back. Clumped together, we step back from the gate and wait, not saying a word. I feel the touch of our bodies pinned against one another. The intimacy of our fear, the smell of adrenaline and sweat steams up from our cluster.

Once we are thoroughly dominated, the horses walk into their corrals for their evening meal. We wait in silence, listening for the horses to settle. Five or ten minutes pass. We can hear the horses chewing on their alfalfa. A few of the men sneak out of our shelter. Hunkered low and moving like thieves, they run to the corrals and shut the gates. I hear the latches slap tight. Now we can reenter our world; the giant beasts are content and contained for the night.

PEOPLE SAY THAT horses mirror their owners. To protect themselves, they become you. They blend themselves to the inside of a person: emotional camouflage. The ranch horses have seen a lot of damaged people over the years. They carry their life stories on their faces, in their postures, and within their unique styles of movement. This physical expression is a language the horses are well equipped to understand. Fear and its family members—anger, frustration, pain—are all carried in the residents' steps, in their shoulders and necks, the way their backs round forward, forcing them to look out through the tips of their eyes, hiding in the shadows just beneath their eyebrows.

Some of the residents move with an artificial confidence, their arms gesturing wildly as they shout orders at their work crew.

Others have no life left in their bodies. They are soft and amorphous, like small sea creatures clinging to a reef. Movement, and the lack thereof, is an emotional story. It tells all. Over the many years this contained engagement between hurting humans and these once-wild animals has created a disaster. Strong men and women beaten down by poverty, by family history, by the prison system, all walk the ranch daily, unknowingly communicating their pain to the horses.

With their ears and eyes, even while grazing head down, the horses see all, feel all. Horses survive by acknowledging risk and by assigning leadership. Flight, not fight, is how horses naturally resolve troubling situations. Leaders become leaders by keeping the herd out of harm's way, by noticing peril and using their inherited gift of speed to reduce the danger posed. Flight or fight. Inside the tall adobe walls of this contained ranch, thousands of years of inherited instinct have been reversed. Lacking the space to truly flee, living among one hundred men and women who broadcast danger with every movement, the horses have chosen to fight.

IT IS MY second trip to the ranch and all the horses are resting inside the woodshop. Six of us go into the woodshop banging on the trash-can lids. The horses panic and run out the double doors. They shoot past the enclosed garden where the radishes and peas spike through the soil, and through the twelve-acre pasture kept for the horses in the middle of the property. Marcus and Rex grab four cuts of alfalfa and head toward the round pen, a recently built structure, seventy feet in diameter. They peel the cuts of alfalfa apart and spread them across the pen. Marcus pulls the gate to the round pen wide open. He's dressed in his running sneakers and sweatpants, with a short-sleeved T-shirt that has *Carolina Panthers* written across it. Once the hay is spread, Marcus and Rex run behind the cottonwood tree for safety. The horses thunder across the pasture and run straight into the pen, devouring the alfalfa as quick as they can. Rex runs from behind the cottonwood and slams the gate shut.

The horses circle the pen, walking from pile to pile, like wild animals sniffing scat. They watch us, their ears flicking back and forth. The livestock crew gathers. Their eyes are dim with what looks like fatigue. They shuffle from task to task wearing over-sized jeans that drape over their work boots. Sarah and Flor huddle away from the men. They, too, look tired, a slate-black tinge under their eyes. I wonder what it must be like to live here on this ranch of mostly men. So far, I've encountered only three other women. I met them briefly in the driveway as I drove in today.

As they lean against the top rail of the pen, the six men from livestock start talking and joking, berating each other over something that happened at breakfast. I watch them from my truck where I gather my rope and a thin bamboo pole. Their attention is not on the horses, it is only on themselves. I realize, as I take a sip of water, that I'll be working alone today.

What I see in these horses worries me. Vigilant and dismissive. Defensive and certain. They know they are contained, but they are far from domesticated.

Without saying a word, I climb over the top rail and begin to work. I choose the big bay named Hawk. Hawk, I was told, was the worst of the herd. He would lead the charge after lunchtime when the residents brought out the trash. Hawk was well versed in trampling and intimidation. Baring his teeth, flattening his ears, and reeling around with his hind legs, he threatened to kick anyone who lingered near his garbage.

When Hawk walks, I walk. When he stops, I stop. He hears

me. His ear and the corner of his eye are sternly on me. The
other horses rummage around the pen from one flake of alfalfa
to another, while Hawk and I walk the perimeter. I pick up my
bamboo cane in my left hand and start tapping it on the ground
as I walk. Hawk's ears flatten. Still walking away from me, he
becomes more and more agitated. He swings his head and neck
toward me like a lion, warning me to back away. The men fall to
a hush, but I keep tapping.

I won't get back, I say in my mind. *No, I will not back up*. Tap.
Tap. Tap. I know what is coming. I have seen it before, but only
rarely. Hawk is about to attack me, and I'm armed with only a
bamboo cane and a thin rope.

First, he charges me halfway. Swinging his shoulders, neck,
and head in my direction. Baring his teeth, ears flat. I stab the
bamboo cane into the center of his chest, then follow with a
quick slap against his bulging pectoral muscles. He flashes himself backward in surprise. I tap against the ground, then swing
the pole around his side, tapping the dirt close to his hind legs,
to let him know I want him to walk forward again. I spread my
legs and crouch a little, readying myself for the next charge. The
rest of the herd shies away from us, then continues chomping on
their alfalfa.

I begin to swing the rope coiled in my right hand, over and
under, in time with the tapping on the ground. And then Hawk
turns and comes at me with all he has. I smack him across the
forehead with my cane, then twice again in rapid succession
across his shoulders. He rises off his front legs, rearing straight
up into the sky and towering over me, refusing to retreat, pumping his front legs at my head. The sound that comes out of me is
one I've never heard before: it's a roar, fierce, determined, and
clear. But I'm trembling. I thrash at his front legs with the bam-

boo, moving sideways but never backward, holding my ground. Down he comes and, on the way, he swings his rear end toward me, aiming. My rope is eight feet long, the lash of it stinging him across his back, his loin, his strong rear-end musculature.

I jump left then right, trying to remove myself from his view. I crash against him with all the force I can draw from my small body. I swing my rope and smack, smack with my cane. He kicks out and spins his hind legs around again, tries to square my body in his line of fire. With a burst of effort, I whip my rope and lash him evenly across the back of his hind legs, giving him a good sting. He jumps forward and away from me. A tiny victory. Tap. Tap. Tap. Hawk walks away, ears pinned. I turn and climb over the top rail taking the pressure off—this a reward for his correct behavior. I drop my rope and pole and walk away from the horses. I try to catch my breath, then cover my mouth with my hands. A cold sweat drips down the back of my neck.

The men mob me, whooping and hooting like I've just hit the game-winning basket. They shout over each other, in disbelief at what they have just witnessed, raising and swinging their arms, attempting a faded imitation of Hawk and his giant gestures. I'm not ready for the entertainment. I stand motionless, facing away from Hawk, knowing I must go back in that pen and try to make a friend.

A sudden sadness comes over me, and I know it's not coming just from me. I look around for Sarah and Flor. They are huddled together near the cottonwood tree, about fifty feet away. They've been watching from a distance, holding on to each other. Sarah's face is red with worry. Flor has her mouth clenched. Her lips curl and disappear inside her face. *This is why they called me*, I hear a voice inside my head. The pain on their faces makes me wonder how long they have had to witness these horses' distress.

After a few minutes, I glance back toward Hawk. He's standing alone where I left him, his head low with one leg cocked and resting. His ears are soft and placed lightly to the sides of his head. His whole body looks deflated, far less rigid. His eyes are half-shut, half-asleep. His mouth hangs loose, with his bottom lip in a droop. The other horses mindlessly eat the alfalfa, never looking up. I ask Marcus to open the gate and let the other horses out of the pen. One at a time they walk back to their pasture, calm and casual. Hawk stays resting.

I climb back over the top rail of the pen and stand on the far side facing Hawk. *This is our new herd*, I think, *just you and me*. "If you don't know what number you are," one of my teachers once told me, "then you are number two." Generally speaking, I think humans could learn to be number two more often, but in this situation I don't have that luxury. I walk to the middle of the pen and pick up my pole, standing quiet and waiting. Hawk's head rises a little, his legs straighten. In the corner of his eye there lies a question, a curiosity toward me. I take a step toward his hind legs holding my pole still. A light, clear "click" comes from the edge of my tongue. Hawk's ears capture it and flick back and forth. I take one more step forward, one more "click." Hawk steps forward and moves away from me. I follow behind at a safe distance. When he slows his step, I "click" and he returns to walking. When I stop, he stops. When I go, he goes. His breath becomes deep and noticeable. He blows out a long and wet tumble of air that cascades out his wide nostrils, then down toward the ground. His mouth and jaw roll his tongue around, he licks his lips. He is giving me a sign that he accepts me. I stop again and walk away, climbing out of the pen. I head over to the dusty old box that holds the halters and pick one out.

Will you let me put this on? Can I get that close? Are you ready?

I walk toward Hawk's shoulder. He sidesteps away from me and curls his neck, staring at the black halter and red lead line like he's looking at a hissing snake.

Whatever happened to you before, it will never happen again.

I jingle the buckle on the halter. Hawk takes a few more steps away but doesn't leave me. I reach out with my right hand and lightly scratch his withers, his shoulder, the middle of his chest. I move my arm up toward his face, his ears, scratching and humming a simple, wordless tune. His eyes soften. The halter now in my left hand, I pull it under and around to the other side where I rub, jingle, and hum some more. He doesn't move away. Hawk is good; he's comfortable. I pull the halter over his neck and bring it behind his ears. I lift it up and over his muzzle, buckle the bridle, and leave the lead line dangling over my left shoulder.

Hawk stiffens when he feels the first tug under his chin. He braces his head upward and hops off the ground with his front legs giving a trivial effort to defy me. I bend his neck around and massage him just behind his ears. I lay my hand across the bridge of his nose and wiggle his head back and forth until it drops closer to the ground. I step forward. He follows, one slow step at a time. We walk around and then out of the pen, in the direction of his other herd. When we reach the pasture's edge, I slide the halter off Hawk. We stand in silence as I groom him with the palm of my hand. Then, as I turn to leave, he bends his head down for the grasses. His left eye follows me into the corner of its socket, trying to keep me in his view.

STRAY DOGS

March / 2013

I leave the horse pasture, gather my bamboo pole and rope from the round pen, and walk toward the corrals. The men have gone back to their dorm rooms to clean up. Sarah and Flor have left for the kitchen. The smell of food cooking sinks into the cool evening air. I throw my rope and pole onto the back seat of my truck and walk the ranch road toward the dining hall. The sun is high, it's five o'clock, and sweat clings to my skin. I wipe my face with the clean edge of my shirttail and tuck the whole hem neatly into my jeans.

Looking around, I don't see any residents. I walk toward a cluster of buildings that are at least one hundred years old. There is not one crack in the old adobe walls. A landscape of simple desert plants surrounds the buildings, and two R. C. Gorman sculptures wrap around a small water fountain near a courtyard. A tall grove of cottonwood trees creates a lush shade over the buildings.

When I push open the dining hall door, chile stings my eyes. I stand in the doorway, watching platefuls of food pass by with fresh tortillas stacked on top, staring out at a room full of eighty to ninety men. Every one of them is dressed in a suit and tie, with their hair cut meticulously short, trimmed tight around their ears. Most have missing teeth and tattoos drawn up their necks, next to their eyes, scrolled across their foreheads. Names like "Lisa" scripted in ink at an angle, behind their ears.

Rex walks over and greets me. He beams down at me from his long, tall frame and I remember how he so willingly unbuttoned his shirt last Sunday to show me the hoof-shaped bruise on his chest. His face is clean-shaven, the sclera around his green eyes white as snow. As far as I can tell, he's the only man so far not covered in tattoos. He shakes my hand and leads me to a table with a sign sitting on top that reads "Livestock."

"Everyone is still cleaning up. They'll be here soon," he tells me.

I nod and smile at him as I sit down. I can feel the cracks of my sunburned lower lip split open as I fake a feeling of calm. The table is huge and so is the room. The space feels swollen with men: moving, sitting, talking, and eating. The clamor of plates and voices bounces off the low ceiling, built in traditional southwestern patterns of thin latillas thatched across enormous round poles, called vigas, which are sixteen inches thick. It seems everywhere I look the men are staring back at me.

Flor and Sarah told me earlier today that they would be part of the team cooking tonight's meal. It is their "tribe's" turn to cook this Sunday, they had said. They're honoring a long-lasting ranch ritual to have a formal dinner once a week. Much like my own family did, many years ago, when my grandparents were still alive. They had invited me to join them and I agreed before asking any questions. I should have asked questions. I should have asked what formal meant. This room full of well-dressed men has my stomach turning. I'm dirty and have a faint hint of horse urine stuck to my boots, which I can smell over the flood of food. My shirt cuffs are stained orange from working horses in the clay of a different ranch. I haven't been home since early this morning. My wind-whipped hair is tangled and stringy against my skinny, dried-out face. It's the way I look at the end of every day. I self-consciously try to comb my fingers through the knots and roll up my sleeves to conceal the stains. My stomach gurgles and sends acid up my esophagus. I sit back in my chair and fold my hands. Try to remember to breathe.

"Listen up, everyone. We have a guest this evening." Rex stands in front of the room and speaks loud enough to quiet the crowd. "Ginger Gaffney is joining us for dinner. She is the horse trainer who has come to help us with our horses. Everyone, please welcome her." With that, the men stand and form a line that quickly swings in my direction.

"Thank you for coming, Ginger." The first man in line reaches out to shake my hand. "My name is Alan. We are grateful for your help."

Alan is tiny. His head might come up to my shoulders. The knot on his tie is loose and folded backward. The cuffs on his suit coat come down past his wrists, to the middle of his hands. I glance down and see the hem of his pants dragging the ground. I stand up to greet him, and remain standing, greeting those in line for the next twenty minutes. Every man in the room comes over to shake my hand and tell me their name. It's a parade of faces and bodies, of smells and touch, of ink drawn on wrinkled skin, of shame and pride. The urine on my boots seems to drift up into each handshake. I feel the shape of my eyes and mouth change with each new man. I'm like a mood ring. Our hands squeeze, and I feel the texture of skin. The firmness of contact carries its own emotion, its own language. At first, the grip of their hands feels coarse, like holding a hammer. Then it softens into flesh on flesh, and we fit together like well-worn gloves. I see the folds of crescent moons form around the corners of their eyes when I smile at them.

Some of the men are seasoned and professional. They've been on this ranch long enough that they know how to greet and be greeted. Others fake it. The most recent arrivals can't look me in the eye. They are the stray dogs scraping for food and running for cover. I often feel like a stray dog when I meet new people. I'm a coward, but I'm hungry. I'm curious. This roomful of men intimidates me. I'm uncomfortable, and I'm fascinated. This balance of opposites always draws me in.

When I finally finish the formal greetings, I sit back down. The men from livestock have come to join me at the table. To my right, left, and across the table, I see the faces of the men who watched as I worked with Hawk this afternoon. The low-hanging chandeliers begin to dim and every man in the room rises to their feet on cue. I follow like I'm at church. From the corner of a hallway that seems to lead toward the kitchen, ten women walk out into the front of the room, all dressed in kitchen whites with differing shades of red chile splattered on their aprons. I recognize Sarah and Flor through their hairnets. All eighty-some men give them a standing ovation. The women beam back at them. One of the women walks forward and announces the meal they have prepared: fresh tortillas, frijoles with guacamole, carne asada, and calabacitas. More cheers erupt from the men, with fist bumps and high fives waving around the crowd. Then the men sit down, and the servers pile out from the hallway with more loaded plates of food.

"You must be hungry, Miss Ginger?" the man to my left asks me.

He is the short, quick one. Thin and agile. I remember him from last Sunday's gathering. He ran out from the shelter like a second baseman, crouched over and bent at the knee. The hay looked like a glove in his hand, swinging side to side as he ran. Then, in one fluid swoop, he tossed the hay into the trough and ran back toward us still bent down from his waist.

"I'm starving," I say. "Haven't had much to eat today. But I'm sorry, can you tell me your name again?" I reach out to shake his hand. "Hey, guys, all of you, can you remind me of your names, please? And maybe, while we wait for our food, can you tell me a little about yourselves? How you got here?"

"I'm Omar," the young man to my left says. "But I don't think we're supposed to talk about ourselves, Miss Ginger. Our pasts, you know, how we got here."

"I think we can tell her. She's not one of us. I'll go check with James and be right back." Rex gets up from the table and walks to the front left side of the room, to a table filled with men much older than everyone else.

"Who's James?" My eyes follow Rex across the room to the table of six men who all turn around and stare at us while Rex leans over to ask his question. I see one man nod a quick yes, then turn back to his plate of carne asada.

"James is the boss, along with that guy sitting right next to him. His name is Daniel. They make all the decisions around here. They've been here the longest." The man sitting across from me stands, then reaches out to shake my hand. "I'm sorry; I forgot to introduce myself. I'm Paul." I notice the wrist brace he is wearing. He's the one Hawk trampled a few weeks ago.

As he leans across the table toward me, I see his broad shoulders and thick chest muscles stretch his suit coat tight across his torso. He takes my hand softly into his and looks straight through me with his piercing dark-brown eyes. "My family has been in prison for four generations," Paul tells me as he holds my hand as gently as if he were holding a kitten. "I'll be the first to get out and stay out." He still has my hand in his. He's still leaning across the table. I take a deep breath and we both nod our heads in agreement.

"Yes. You will be the first. And let the others in your family follow your lead." I don't know where that thought came from, but it shot out of my mouth before I could stop it.

On my first visit, Sarah and Flor had told me this whole ranch is run by addicts and felons. I couldn't understand at first, but now I see it. Everyone in this room has lived a life of trouble.

"It's cool," Rex says on his return and sits down. "James said to keep our stories short."

"I'll go next. My name is Marcus. I've been here for almost two years. I have three more months till I can start working out."

"Working out?" I question, hoping for an explanation.

"Once we are finished with our term, we are given four more months to go into town and get a job. Make some money and return to the ranch every night to check in. It's a test period, to see how we'll do."

The servers interrupt and lay massive plates of food in front of us. Nobody reaches for a fork. I'm thinking about Marcus. His words and his body don't match. His eyes dart around the room as he speaks, while his knees pop up and down in a rapid, nervous twitch. He's clean-cut and speaks well. But I wonder how he will do holding down a job, five days a week, eight hours a day. Is his sobriety strong enough to hold up to that pressure? Being sober and drug-free looks like this new suit he's wearing—not yet worn in.

"Let's eat," I say. Everyone picks up their forks and digs in. Flor and Sarah arrive at the table, and everyone slides down a chair on either side to make room. They are still dressed in their white kitchen clothes, the messy kitchen aprons removed.

"This looks fucking awesome!" A large man sitting to the far left side of the table chomps on his homemade tortilla. "You gals get the award. Best fuckin' meal this month."

"Thanks, Randy," Flor and Sarah reply in unison. They are a beautiful team in their white uniforms, with their hair freshly combed and out of their hairnets. They sit quiet and take in the compliments. Both are bright-eyed. I can see why they've been chosen to head the livestock crew. They don't know much about horses, but they know how to get things done and work as a team. I've worked on plenty of ranches where those two skills never managed to come together.

"Hey, I'm Randy." The man still chomping his tortilla turns and faces me. "I'm not supposed to be here. I already served my time. Four years in that fuck hall. It's my wife; she sent me here. After my last release, she told me to get control over my anger, or else. I got me a daughter who's a senior in high school this year. She's smart. On the honor-ey role. She's gonna be speaker, the val-dic-tor-an of her class. She graduates in May. I fuckin' won't be there." Randy drops his fork in his calabacitas and leans over his plate.

"Keep it short, Randy," Rex cuts him off. "I'm in voluntarily, also." Rex turns and faces me. A not-too-wide smile forms on his face. "Been here six months so far." He takes a long breath, looks past me, and gathers himself. "I just started with the horses when Paul got hurt. I'm grateful you're here to help us."

"So, what made you come here instead of, you know, some other rehab facility?" I ask him.

"I've been to five rehab facilities. Nothing held." He looks down at his boots and shuffles them around for no apparent reason. "I finally, finally knew—I was going to die an addict. If I quit using, I would die. If I kept using, I would die. This is my last shot at staying alive. I know now that I can't do it on my own."

"This ranch is our family, our home," Flor breaks in. "We work together, reach out to each other when we're struggling. Most of us don't have a family that can help us change. We've run them off or they're addicts themselves."

I want to ask Flor about her family, what happened to her that made her choose drugs. I stop myself. I think about my own life. All the wrong turns I have made. How lucky I was just to be sitting here, acting as if I could actually be of some help.

Sarah works her way through the pause in our conversation. "That's my story. My family doesn't want anything to do with me. I'm a flunky. I've been in and out of prison and rehab centers my whole life. I'm just grateful the judge sent me here this last time. I hope it sticks."

She's shaking like a leaf in the wind as she speaks. I want to reach out and hold her. But, God, I know I can't. I feel myself getting dragged into her pain, into everyone's pain. I felt it with Hawk earlier, and now again. I pull my chair up against my back for support and collect my ponytail into a tighter knot. I need to do something with my nervous hands.

"And what brought you here?" The voice comes from across the far left side of the table. This man has kept his distance all day, folding his arms across his chest and staring away from me whenever I spoke to the group. These are the first words I've heard him speak since I began working Hawk early this afternoon.

"You gonna teach us something about horses?" he ask.
lips pinch together in a smirk, and his head jiggles like a pla
doll in a rearview mirror.

"And you are?" I ask.

"I'm Tony, and I'm a junkie. I've done some stupid fucked-up
things that no one needs to hear about. But what I want to know
is what are *you* gonna teach us about these horses? You some kind
of whisperer or whatever?" It is obvious he isn't asking a question.
Randy laughs hard and chokes on his tortilla. He takes a big gulp
of tea and laughs some more. Tony joins in and cracks a grin. It's
an inside joke. No one else at the table joins them.

"What the fuck is wrong with you guys?" Paul looks down the
table at them, then back up to Flor and Sarah.

"Yeah, like you two could do better than Ginger did today?"
Sarah stands up, leans over the table, and shouts at Tony and
Randy. "Take your sarcastic attitude and keep it to yourself. We
don't need it."

Suddenly every man in the room is staring at our table.

"It's alright," Flor says. "Sit down, Sarah."

"You think she can catch them? We've had more than ten men
at a time out there trying to catch them. How's she going to do
it? That's what I wanna know." Tony is talking directly to Flor.

"Catch who?" I ask.

"There are two more horses you haven't met yet," Flor confesses. "They've been here for two years, and no one has been
able to catch them. One is hurt, real bad."

"Where are they?"

"They live behind the building we call Headquarters. We feed
them there and keep water for them. Once, we tried to run them
into a corral. But that's when the accident happened. That's when
she got hurt."

I ask with concern.

split open and filled with pus," Sarah

they tell me this sooner? I scoot my rear to the

my seat, lean back in my chair, and hold my forehead

the palm of my hand. How in the world could it take two years to catch a horse? I drop my head forward and I stare at the ground. I let out a sigh.

"Have you contacted a veterinarian?" I ask Sarah.

"Yeah. But he can't catch them, either." Sarah sits forward in her chair and bends around Omar to look me in the eye. "That's why we called you. We got your number off a flyer at the Española feed store."

I had wondered where she and Flor had gotten my number. I look up into Sarah's pink-cheeked face. Her hand is cupped over her mouth with worry.

"We can catch them, Ginger, I know it," Flor tells me. Her voice certain and clear, no doubt lingers in her inflection.

I'm swelling with doubt. Am I the right person for this? Hawk almost nailed me earlier today, a number of times. How many more of their horses are going to be that dangerous? I must be careful with my body; it's how I make my living. Not to mention that I'm fond of being alive. No one has offered to pay me. No one on the ranch makes any money. Should I really keep coming? Maybe I could refer them to a different trainer and leave it at that. But who would come if they aren't getting paid?

"Are they both mares?" I ask Flor. She's out of her seat, waiting for me to respond.

"Sisters," she tells me. "They came together. Were dropped off without halters or anything."

The sun is dropping behind the western Jemez mountains. A

blaze of orange and red fills the parking lot outside the dining hall. Little bubbles in the handmade glass windowpanes turn into tiny, blood-red balls, filling the room with rose-colored light.

The servers take our plates and return with trays of warm biscochitos, drizzled with sugar on top. We stop our conversations and reach for a few of the warm treasures.

"I'll have to come back." The back of my throat is raw with restraint as I chew on one of the cookies.

"When?" Tony asks. "I wanna make sure I'm here for this."

"I'll be back in a few days. Don't feed them. We need those mares hungry."

"Why do they need to be hungry?" Rex asks with genuine curiosity.

"Cause we'll need to bait them into the round pen if we can. Don't feed them. No one feeds them. You'll have to let everyone know that those horses get no food. You understand?"

Everyone nods their heads in agreement.

I pause for a minute, gaze around the table, and take a long, slow breath. "Flor, Sarah, and I will do this alone," I tell them. "I'll let you know when I need the rest of your help."

I get up from the table. Tony rolls his eyes. The rest of the men rise with me.

"Thank you for inviting me." I look toward Flor and Sarah. "I'll give you a call. Check with you in a few days."

"I'll get the key to the gate and let you out, Miss Ginger." Omar moves ahead of me. He walks over to the front desk and asks for the keys. I stand next to the dining hall door and say goodbye to the men sitting at the closest table to the exit.

"Please come back. You can have dinner with us anytime," a few of the men tell me as I'm leaving.

The door shuts behind me. I hear voices, plates, forks, and

knives muffle from inside the adobe walls. I'm shaking my head in disbelief as I walk to my truck. I've seen a lot of people and a whole mess of horses that need my help. But I've never seen anything like this. On my way through the gate, I wave goodbye to Omar. He waves back at me with an open-toothed smile. I turn left out the gate and head north toward home but feel something tugging at me, something chained to the ground.

MOON AND STAR

March / 2013

Luna's wound site is swollen and full of pus. Her right eye shut and padded, like an overstuffed pillow. It looks like it's ready to blow. There's a trickle of yellow oozing from the corner, where the infection has sunk beneath the surface of a five-inch zigzag crack blazing across the center of her face. Without some attention and a long round of antibiotics, Luna will lose that eye.

Other than her swollen face, Luna's on her A game. She and her sister Estrella, both black-and-white Paint Horses, have roamed free on this seventeen-acre ranch, uncatchable for the last two years. The ranch residents have chased them into every corner, every structure, even into this seventy-foot round pen. No one's been able to lay a hand on them. Sarah told me what happened to Luna in our phone call last night. One of the residents, a part-time team roper, part-time drug smuggler from Las

Cruces, ran Luna into a stall one afternoon six weeks ago and tried to rope her. His loop fell halfway across her face as she reared up and smacked her head on the twelve-inch overhanging shelter beam. Blood splattered everywhere as Luna shot out of the shelter, knocking the cowboy off his feet and catching her left hip on a T-post. Her flank sliced open like two pink lips parting.

They've had the veterinarian out two different times attempting to treat her. But no luck.

Today Luna and Estrella are hungry. Everyone has followed my instructions, skipping two days of feed so we can bait the mares into the round pen, lock the gate, then try to catch them. Sarah shakes a bucket of grain, tempting them out from the alleyway behind the tall building where they seem to find security. She walks across desert weeds, dropping small piles of grain, hoping to lure the sisters across the field and over toward the round pen. The New Mexico sun is already high in the sky, and it's only midmorning. Estrella moves out in front of Luna and gobbles up the piles. Pieces of rolled oats fall from her mouth as she chews sideways and carelessly. Luna shoves her head to the ground to eat what Estrella has left behind. Pile by pile, they walk slow and steady across the field toward the pen. Until now, Flor and I have stayed hidden inside the hay barn. As they approach, Flor walks to the round pen with two fat flakes of alfalfa. Luna and Estrella raise their heads and watch as Flor opens the gate and places the flakes against the farthest wall. She turns and hurries back into the barn. Sarah advances. Her luring piles of grain are now farther apart. She takes what's left in the bucket and pours it into the center of the pen. We open the gate and Sarah joins us in the hay barn.

Estrella comes through the gate first, like a wildcat, slowly lifting each hoof from the knee. She holds her leg up with just enough pause that it looks as though she's ready to pounce on a kill. Muzzle to the ground, her back arching high, her hindquarters dig in and sink under her body. She drops her head into the pile of grain. Sarah, Flor, and I watch from inside the barn, about one hundred feet from the pen. Luna enters aslant. She twists and turns in every direction, certain that trouble follows her everywhere. She bends over the bright green leaves of the alfalfa with a wary backward twitch of her ears. Sarah moves out from the barn with long, quiet steps and snaps the round pen gate closed behind them.

We move in closer and watch the sisters silently pick at the clover-sized leaves. The far reaches of their upper lips acting like fingertips, dragging the miniature leaves onto their tongues. Luna's body trembles as she eats. We can see the shake of it across her topline where her long winter hairs bristle and shimmy across her spine. Estrella lets out a wet blow from her muzzle and continues chewing on the alfalfa. She's smaller and less athletic. With a short back and barreled belly, she almost looks pregnant. The hollowed-out dish in her nose tells me she is at least part Arabian.

Sarah and Flor talk in whispers, hashing out some drama that happened in the women's dorm last night. There are only ten women on this ranch—from what I've been told—all of whom come from women-only prisons. There is no such thing as a coed prison, and for good reason. Flor and Sarah have both mentioned to me that living with eighty or so men on this small ranch is one of the hardest things to navigate. Both men and women are constantly getting in trouble for messing around.

Flor looks down at her hands and spreads each finger out wide, admiring her multicolored fingernails that match the red and purple ribbons woven into her long, ponytailed braid. There's already a chip in two of her nails, and we haven't even started yet. They huddle over this major disappointment as I break their reverie and remind them exactly why we're here today.

Sarah has a wayward leg that curls out to the side of her body like a pirate's hook. With each stride, the right side of her body collapses. I worry over how to keep them safe. We must enter this round pen like wolves: intimidating, fierce, demanding respect and accepting nothing less. Sarah is chewing on her cuticles as if they are question marks, and Flor twists the end of her braid over and over.

"Flor, you ready?"

"Absolutely."

"You sure?"

Flor explained in our first meeting that she's a compulsive liar. She can't tell the truth from a lie. She's been that way most of her life. Around this ranch, she said, they call it false pride. But, for Flor, it's more than that. She has a thin hold on what's real and what's not. Her many years of heroin addiction make knowing the difference difficult.

I pause, and she recognizes I'm waiting for her to pay better attention, to forget about her ponytail, her fingernails, and return to the business at hand.

"I'm not sure if I'm ready, Miss Ginger. What would you like us to do?"

"I need you both to bend your knees; spread your arms and legs out wide; make yourselves bigger. Watch me." I bend down into a practiced basketball position, spread my skinny frame out as far as it will go, and start to slide sideways—right to left, then left to right, my arms stretched and flapping like flags. "We're going to have to work as a team in there, one unit, no holes. If they see any space between us, they will try to break through."

To my right, Sarah crouches and starts to slide with me; Flor slides on my left. With our outstretched arms and legs, we entwine ourselves into a human wall. Straight and woven but still not strong enough to separate these mares.

"We need to practice. Flor, stand over there next to the cottonwood tree, please. Sarah, you can stay near the round pen. Bend your knees and take your positions. No matter what crazy shit I do, don't back away."

They laugh but know I'm not joking. Flor shifts her stance wide but gets distracted by a loose shoestring. Sarah can't stop sucking and picking at her fingers. Neither of them know what's coming, nor do they know what to expect next. They listen, then they refocus. Flor bobs up and down on the toes of her sneakers, trying to prepare herself. Sarah sighs, then bunches her fingers into fists. She bends slightly from her waist and brings her fists close to her chin like a boxer.

I run down the road about a hundred feet from them and ask again if they're ready. They give me half nods, and I haul up the road right at Flor. Screaming, growling, pinning my upper lip to the bottom side of my nostrils. Flor sits low in her stance with her arms out in front, elbows bent, primed to defend herself against my attack. As I get close, she breaks forward at me and yips a cold sound that cracks from the narrow part of her throat. Her spit hits my face like a switch. Now, directly in front of her, I howl an angry call, jump up and down, and try my best to fill up with fury. Flor returns a pitchy scream that sends pins and needles into my ears, followed by two big stomps close to my toes. The earthy smell of her breath anchors me. Sarah turns her head away and covers her face with her hands. Our staged version of a cockfight has her backtracking. Flor's arms swing wild, elbows knocking at mine. Luna and Estrella have stopped eating and run to the far side of the pen.

I look over at Sarah, who's beading up a sweat. "Please don't do that to me," she says.

I drop my arms to my waist and turn to address Sarah. She removes her hands from her face and says, "Maybe, maybe I'm not the right person for today."

Her legs are shaking. I can see that my practice session with Flor has sent Sarah into some old trauma. I walk toward her, speaking slow and calm.

"You are the right person. You certainly are, just stick close to me." I wave them both together and bring them in front of me. "We're ready."

I watch as Flor and Sarah walk ahead of me toward the round pen. They look like a moving puzzle, broken pieces stuck momentarily together. I wonder how long we can hold our wall intact. Estrella and Luna's ears follow us as we get closer. They run around the pen at a slow trot. Their bodies move and curve like a school of fish, neat and tucked, swinging in unison with each stride. I hear the crunch of gravel under my feet. I try to relax my shoulders. We must be whole for this to work. The horses will see us for who we are. We'll have no secrets, no lies to protect us. Just the honesty of our bodies.

WE ENTER THE round pen and latch the gate behind us. The two mares fly around the perimeter in a panic. Luna is out in front, with Estrella close behind. Flor and Sarah are positioned off the wings of my shoulders, arms and legs spread out wide, forming the needle of a rotating dial, a solid line across the center of the pen. Sarah and I walk forward as Flor moves backward, turning our needle counterclockwise. When the mares turn up their pace, our walking turns into a run.

We're looking for a large enough gap between the sisters' bodies to step in and slice the two apart, put our woman-made wall between them and break their bond. Flor sees an opening and slides sideways into the break, turning Estrella back to the right while Luna keeps spinning left. The separation cuts our pen and the sisters into two. All hell breaks loose.

Estrella turns back and forth. She tries to return to Luna, who screeches a piercing note that travels across the pasture and bounces off the twelve-foot adobe ranch walls. Our needle turns as fast as Estrella. The two sisters peel around their separate spheres in a frenzy. The small pen makes our frames look larger than we are. Every turn Estrella makes sends our needle spinning in the opposite direction.

Behind us, Luna's in a tantrum. From the corner of my eye, I catch glimpses of her stomping her front hooves to the ground, then rearing toward the sky, thrashing out with her front legs. Flor holds hard to her position, running forward then backward at Estrella's every turn. Her breath speaks in grunts. The needle spins round and round as our bodies struggle to keep our human wall in place. Sarah is tiring. Her arms and legs shrinking closer to her body as her energy wanes. She's crossing her legs behind instead of sliding, tripping herself up on each rotation.

Estrella swoops back to the right and our needle whirls around with her. Sarah loses her balance and is down on one knee. Estrella finds the hole. She breaks through the rift in our wall and gallops back to Luna, catching Sarah's crooked leg and knocking her face-first to the ground. Luna's screaming halts. The mares meet up and flank each other, two bodies becoming one.

Luna's roars have pulled in a crowd. Residents gather from all around the ranch. In my peripheral vision, I see some of the men from livestock arrive: Rex, Paul, and Omar. Tony and Randy are nowhere to be seen. The men lean into the upper rail of the pen and start asking questions. Their curiosity causes a deep distraction for Flor and Sarah. Sarah picks herself up and slaps at the dust covering her right side. Her face is covered in a pink shade of brown, and her forehead is scraped and pocked with small pebbles. A contagion of adrenaline starts to swirl around us. A mindless fever. A thousand black starlings cackling into the sky.

"Quiet, quiet!" I call out. "You are welcome to stay, but please be quiet. And step back, please, two feet from the rail."

I set the boundaries, and everyone comes to a hush while Flor, Sarah, and I return to our positions. I can see doubt forming on their faces, like maybe we won't be able to do this, won't be able to catch them or halter them. We won't be able to separate them and clean Luna's wound. Sarah looks at the ground and kicks at the dirt. Flor hasn't spoken a word since the crowd gathered.

"Are you two alright?" I walk over to Sarah, put my hand on her shoulder, and check the gashes in her forehead. "We can stop if you need to," I say, "and start again tomorrow." Flor walks over and stands so close I feel the heat of her body rise onto my face.

"I'm not stopping. No way. Look at her." She juts her chin at Luna. "We've gotta help her—today." We turn toward Luna and see the yellow pus drooling across her cheek. Flor's arms are relaxed and down by her sides. Her breath is even, and she holds her head at such a tilt I can see her nostrils flaring in and out. She's calm; she's confident; she's ready.

Sarah agrees. We get back into our positions, which sends the sisters rushing around the perimeter of the pen. Luna leads once again. Estrella dragging behind now. She's tiring. Her footfalls are no longer fueled by panic and fear. Flor steps into the slot and cuts her back to the right; the connection between Estrella and Luna is broken, again.

Sliding together, long strokes, we move as a band of feral horses. The space between our bodies swells with purpose. We push Luna's torment into the back of our minds as Estrella starts to change. She's running half rounds now, pivoting off our cue as we swing our needle left to right, right to left in a syncopated dance. A quiet balance comes over her. She runs for five more minutes and stops, parallel with the rail, breathing heavy, both eyes facing us. I see something familiar in her face. Her wildness disrobed, her domestic breeding peeking through.

We stay motionless and let Estrella rest. Her body quivers, muscles loosening their grip. Her mind begins to untie itself from Luna. I move toward her from the center of the ring. If she is to take a step or try to bolt, Flor and Sarah have my corners and can cut her back. I reach out to touch her, scratch her neck and shoulders, the middle of her chest. She sucks in a half-caught gulp and then blows out the extra with one soft snort.

Flor and Sarah are overwhelmed with emotion. Tears catch on their lower lashes. They have lived a long time on this ranch, unable to touch these mares. This ranch is small. Every person and every animal is tied to the whole. Luna and Estrella have been on their own, isolated and traumatized, for far too long. Flor and Sarah know what it's like to live that way.

We keep an eye out for Luna, who's pacing back and forth in the other half of the pen, pitching a mournful wail every few strides. I leave Estrella and hustle to the box that holds the purple and red halters Flor has picked out for today, the same colors as her fingernails. I take soft steps back to Estrella and resume my hand massage with the halter and lead line draped over my shoulder.

Without even the slightest flinch, Estrella lets me slide the noseband over her muzzle. I latch the brass buckle, and Estrella follows behind as I move toward the gate. I know now that Estrella has been handled by humans before she came to this ranch. She accepts my touch, offers a quick sense of trust. Horses who are damaged don't make these changes with ease. Luna has stopped her desperate calls and, for the first time, stands quiet and watches Estrella walk away. Everything is crisp, clean, silent. I gesture for Flor to come get Estrella. We change places.

At a slow walk, Sarah, Flor, and Estrella exit the pen. Estrella's head and neck are low and swing loose from her body. Her eyes are round glassy marbles. They no longer glance sideways looking for trouble. I'm amazed how fast she can change families. It carves a piece of loneliness from the middle of my chest. As they stride out together, I notice Sarah's limp is gone. Her bent leg is straight as a walking cane.

I turn and widen my stance, waiting for Luna to burst toward her sister as she leaves the pen, but Luna is motionless, standing parallel to the rail on the opposite side of the pen. Her one good eye, a shotgun.

Flor told me how the sisters arrived at the ranch two years ago. They were dropped here by a small-time breeder from a nearby town.

"They're too small," he told the livestock crew. But what he meant was, they're mares. People like geldings. Neutered males bring a higher price and sell easily.

No one from livestock knew enough to look in the trailer, to see if they had halters on, to ask the man if they'd been handled before. They swung open the trailer door while the owner banged on the side walls with a stick, trying to frighten the horses out. Luna and Estrella twisted and crashed against each other and then, in a panic, leaped out the back and took off across the pasture, never to be touched again. Until now.

One of the men from livestock asked the owner if they had names.

"They ain't got none. They're sisters, though," the breeder said. He slammed the trailer door and jogged around to the front cab of his truck, wishing them luck as he hurried out the gate, the livestock team in his rearview mirror.

"Flunkies," Sarah told me. "They're flunkies, just like us."

Barely touched. Thinly loved. Not even given a name.

WE ALL COME FROM somewhere, but that does not mean we belong. Sarah's mom tried to strangle her two weeks before she took her own life. Now Sarah stands with her short beefy arms wrapped around Estrella's black-and-white neck, her head pressed into Estrella's forehead. Both close their eyes. Flor pulls down with her fingers and struggles to unravel the tangled knots locked solid into Estrella's mane. Inside my truck, I drink a cold bottle of water, catch my breath, and watch the three of them. About a half dozen men gather around and dote over Estrella. On the back seat of my truck sits the lariat I brought over, hoping I would not need to use it. Resting flat and docile against the fabric, it looks nothing like the noose I may have to float over Luna's neck if I can't catch her.

Luna's no longer crying for her sister, no longer looking up. Her one open eyelid half covers her good eye. She paces around the perimeter, hits the middle of the gate, paces back again. A sick, empty rhythm comes from her hooves. When horses are in distress, they turn inward and ignore the world around them. They look more like robots than animals of prey. No longer alert, their ears fall sideways and face the ground. They move like caged animals, purposeless. They stand still, staring out into the distance, without blinking.

I take another sip of water. My throat begins to burn. I know this sunken place. For the first six years of my life, I rarely spoke. Silence was my inheritance, like my blonde hair and broad forehead. Like the worried wrinkles around my baby eyes. I came into this world choosing to stay mute. I would not speak, not even in the confines of my room. I lived in a dead space, where silence kept me protected. Language was not to me what it is to most people—power to express. Power to understand. To me language sounded like a knife, cutting everything apart.

I was born into a fast-moving family. They talked fast. They moved fast. One paragraph rolled into the next, without a breath. The space to listen, to form a thought, to build a sentence, was infinitesimally small. Every conversation was a simultaneous avalanche of sounds that roared and circled around us, a constant spray of words that seemed to squeeze the air out of the room.

Unable to speak, I learned to watch bodies. My family became a cacophony of motion—fingers, hands, arms, touching, twitching, scratching, and picking. Torsos rocking, twisting away from each other when they got too close. Eyes darting around the room, staring at the ceiling, out the window, downward toward the ocher-colored linoleum floor. Lips that held stiff wrinkles in their corners, always prepped for the clamor of thought waiting to exit their heads.

I sat in the center of this human storm until my torso curled forward into a small ball. I would crawl between their roiling bodies toward the couch where our dog, Sandy, slept. Taking refuge under the living room table that sat in front of the sofa. There I watched. From the knee down, their legs were like the branches of trees caught in violent weather—rubbing, twisting, a snap and crackle of joints. Looking up, I could see Sandy's chest take in long deep breaths, her body a still point where my eyes could rest.

LUNA'S HEAD HAS sunk low to the ground She has quit her pacing and stands shoved up against the corral wall. I lean back, pick up the lariat from the seat of my truck, and walk toward the round pen.

Tony and Randy have arrived and, along with the rest of the men from livestock, they arrange themselves around the outside of the pen, like boulders, just as I begin to make my underhand loop. I'm not great with a lariat. I learned it a number of years ago from an older cowboy. Mostly I take practice swings at a plastic cow's head outside my barn a few days each month. Catching poor terrified Luna will be a much harder target.

Luna's pain enters my body through my eyes and I see what I must do. She will never give herself up. She won't do this on her own. She will fight for her freedom, even if it means losing that eye.

Luna has a break in her. Either she was born with it, or someone put it in her. Either way, she has no home. I'll have to make her come to us. Not ask her, not love her, not try to change her. I'll have to rope her. I'm nervous, but I have no choice. She looks half dead before I start to swing, but then she wakes and takes off in a gallop.

Angles. It's all about angle: three, four, five feet. I've got to think ahead. Step back behind her. Straight across from her and all I'll do is throw this loop right at the side of her face. The loop must come in like an unseen cloud, something that drops in and over her before she knows what has happened. If I miss, if I hit her face with this rawhide hanger, she'll try to break through the walls.

Some of the men have their hands on their hips, legs spread to the width of their bodies, as Luna peels around the pen. Tony and Randy hold their arms out wide, waving them, trying to distract her. She races around the pen in a rage, watching my loop grow. Sweat drips down the back of her legs. Her ears are flat, and her tail is pinched up between her butt cheeks. She's ready to kick the shit out of me if I get too close.

Counting again, my loop grows slow. It's long and narrow, but I need it wider. The front edge of my loop keeps hitting the ground as I swing. I flatten my elbow, move it closer to my body, and straighten my wrist. My hand faces the sky as my loop bloats big enough to cover half her body. One . . . two . . . three, I let it fly. It's coming up from behind her, shoots out in front like a massive Frisbee, and hovers. It's three feet ahead of her and she freaks, kicks herself into fifth gear to outrun it, and the loop drops in around her shoulders.

Take out the slack. Damn it, take out the slack. Don't let it slide down toward her legs and tangle things up. I'm running backward. Coiling my lariat, snatching it up around her neck. I grab the rope with both hands and tuck my arms close to my body, hands out in front of my stomach, ready for her to hit the end. Contact! She's in the air. Her front legs jump above my line, she turns, and the lariat pulls from under her belly. Another hit, and I take her momentum and swing her back the other direction. She's tangled and pissed. She's thrashing her front legs at the line as she gallops around trying to unravel herself. One more revolution around the pen, hopping and bucking, and the rope hangs again from her neck. I coil the lariat tighter, grab hold, and with all 122 pounds of me, I pull her around and she faces me at a halt. Steaming.

She bolts. Again she turns, trying to outrun the connection, but there's nowhere to go. We're tied to each other. Fifteen more minutes of wheeling, back and forth. I'm coiling the lariat in, closer and closer. I have her five feet in front of me at a standstill. I can smell the stench of her infected face from here. I'm not making a friend today. Today we are going to save that eye.

I move off to the side of her, not too close to her hindquarters, and fold her neck around to her rib cage. From this position, she'll have to bend those hindquarters under her body and reface me. From this position, she can't bolt, and she can't level me. I bend her side to side, for ten more minutes, until her neck feels half as stiff. My mouth is dry, my jaw tight, my skin trembles as sweat tingles under my shirt.

"Two men. Two men," I shake the words from the back of my throat. "I need two volunteers. Somebody get the hose hooked up to the hydrant. We need to clean her up."

Tony jumps the round pen wall.

"I can hold her," he says. I have Luna's head bent so close to her body that her muscles are fatigued and shaking. The lariat burns in my hands.

"You can't let her straighten out," I tell Tony. "She'll line her hindquarters up and kick the hell out of you."

"I got the hose!" Rex yells, then pulls the green snaking monster toward Luna. She gurgles and huffs at it like it is going to kill her.

"Slow! Move slow, Rex!" I shout at him, then pump my arms toward the ground to settle his forward motion. "Turn up the water. Just a little at a time, please. We don't need to spook her any more than she is."

I hear the squeaky hydrant handle lift upward and a dribble of water slips from the mouth of the hose.

"Ready, Tony?" I ask.

He nods one quick bump of his head; Rex holds up the end of the hose, and water starts to leak across Luna's face. She twists her head in jerks trying to get loose, opening her mouth then snapping her teeth together. *Clack. Clack. Clack.* Even restrained she's fighting for her life.

"It's only water, Luna," I say in a soft voice, then tell Paul, who's over at the hydrant, to pull the handle up a little farther. Water is pouring over Luna's face. Tony has her in a firm grip. Luna's good eye twitches back and forth, looking for what might come next.

"Turn the water off," I instruct Paul. The hose runs dry. "Tony, with your right hand, can you scratch her a little?" I know if we take this in stages, Luna will learn to trust us.

Tony takes the edge of his fingernails and scratches the bumpy mosquito bites that cover her neck.

"More. Just like that. Keep scratching," I tell him. Tony digs in, and Luna starts to lean in to his touch. She chokes out a cough and green alfalfa leaves spray out of her mouth. Then she licks her lips and swallows. Licks her lips and swallows. Drops her head and sighs.

"Turn on the water, please. Slowly again." Paul turns on the hydrant. Rex places the hose against her face. Luna takes a long, loose breath and allows the water to seep into the deep crack along her forehead. The crusty pus starts to let free, one small chunk at a time, until the larger chunks give way. I walk in closer to see the damage. I can see bone. The edges of the skin around the break are already dead. Blood flow to this area has ceased long ago.

Sarah and Flor come up behind me and breathe on the back of my neck as they stare at the damage. Luna's face looks like a topography map. Layers of pink, gray, and hints of green line the three-inch crack.

"Is she going to be okay?" Flor whispers.

I look around and see their faces leaning in toward Luna's pain.

"I don't know. Just keep the water coming."

SKINLESS

North Carolina / 1992

The sound of frantic hooves fills the night air. She is knee deep in autumn oak leaves raked this afternoon from the east side corner of the old goat shed. Not the best bedding for a high-strung horse, but the only option I had. As I near the barn, I hear the sound of leaves being crunched and flung against the stall wall. The half-moon creates long shadows across the barn lot, spreading the shapes of tree branches on the ground beneath my feet. She stops and listens for me. I peer between the harvested pine boards wrapping around her twelve-by-twelve stall. The boards twist and rise the way old trees grow. With my forehead against the furry splinters of unfinished wood, I see the outline of her body. The arch of her neck meets her back, flowing into a long flat valley before it curves up again over her rump into a low rising hill. She returns to her pacing. Her body twisting around the four corners of her cage.

Tiny branches snap like miniature bombs under her hooves, creating a cascade of tremors that ripple over her taut skin. She blows hard from her chest. Out of her wet nostrils, mist leaks through the space between the boards and tingles my cheeks. The intimacy of it fills me with the same fear I've had with lovers. *How dangerous are you? How close will I have to get to know you?*

She stops in front of me, lowers her head to the height of my gaze, and peers back through the thin space between the boards. We are inches apart, eye level. I try to take a breath. It goes halfway down my throat. I close my lips and the air pushes out my nose in a half-choked grunt. She spooks to the opposite corner, then blows out a cold snort. A high-pitched squeal fills the old barn.

NO ONE THOUGHT I should buy her. Not my lover, nor any of my friends. No one except Bob, whose seventy-acre farm abuts our ten acres and old log cabin. When I asked about keeping a horse at his barn, he went right to work on the old manual water pump, replacing it with a brand-new red one, stiff and squeaky. It demanded fifteen upward tugs and fifteen downward pulls to fill a mere five-gallon bucket of water. It would work itself loose, he said, and then went to oiling it in all the noisy places.

We drove over to meet her in Bob's old farm truck one afternoon after work. A twenty-minute drive west on I-40 and then a turn south on I-85. Driving as fast as the old truck could go, we stayed in the right-hand lane. A steady stream of newer vehicles passed us. Drivers and passengers staring sideways through the truck window as they went by. I wondered, as they stared at me, which woman they saw. The quiet, invisible ghost of myself or the woman I was about to become.

Bob and I talked easily about growing hay the following spring and about the land where he had lived for most of his life. Bringing a horse back onto his land was a silent dream reawakened, a reason to keep up the routine of farming that Bob loved. It gave his life purpose.

We drove onto the pristine horse farm complete with a perky, white fence, a neatly crowned pebbled driveway, and fields of bright-green fertilized grass. The rolling hills were spotted with well-groomed horses wearing lightweight blankets to keep their coats from fading in the sun. The owner had told me the mare was difficult when I first called. They had put a few rides on her, but this horse was far from gentle, the owner said. She had broken out of halters and bridles, knocked down gates, and jumped over fences. I hung up and relayed these brief descriptions to Bob, who wasn't the least bit concerned.

"Ain't no reason we can't get her through all that. She's young," he confided in his sing-song southern voice.

When we arrived, she was in a large stall, halfway down the impeccably clean barn aisle. Not one blade of hay or spotting of manure in sight. We heard her first, blowing short snorts and stomping the ground, rattling the upright bars on her stall walls. Dust poured from her stall into the alley of the barn. I was shocked when I first saw her. She was terrified and angry, sweat all over her body, frothy-white foam bubbling up between her chest muscles. She looked crazed, untamable, as if she'd seen a demon. The young men who worked at the barn greeted us and handed over her halter and bridle. They asked us to be careful, and then they left us alone.

Bob sent me back to his truck, where I pulled out the brushes and combs, hoof pick, saddle blanket, and Bob's old cherished saddle layered in dust. It had a signature handmade stamp on the corner of the skirt. Faint and worn out, it read: *Saddle Maker; Billy Cook.* I stacked all the gear on the outside of her stall. We entered, first unlatching the gate, then the two strands of chains wrapped around the door frame that held tight the barricade they built to keep her from busting free. Steam rose off her back. Her eyes were rounder than harvest moons, lined with a spooky white edge. She danced around us. Her feet barely touching the ground.

"Easy, girl," Bob rolled his words out slow. If he was nervous, there was not one sound or sight of it in him. "E A S Y."

Bob walked right up to her and laid his hand on her shoulder. She stopped her feet as he reached for her, and stood, head high, right next to him. I handed Bob one of the brushes. There wasn't much to clean off her. She was a shimmering bronze red, the metallic color of a newly minted motorcycle. He brushed her anyway. His touch seemed to settle her, to stabilize her instinct to run. He moved the brush along her back and over her loin, then back to her chest, knocking the globs of sweaty foam off her bulging, young muscles. All the while, Bob spoke to her in a soft voice. Bob was hard of hearing and said just about everything in a full-out scream. But he whispered to her like he was in a dream. I imagined he could only hear his own words from the inside of his head, yet the mare heard him just fine. I handed him the mane and tail comb, and he went about his magic, soothing her high anxiety. Her head dropped down as he pulled the comb through her hair.

"We ain't gonna tie her. Ain't no sense in that. She don't need that kind of pressure today," he yelled at me. The mare stood, seemingly unconcerned about his vocal outburst, her ears twitching back and forth. "We're gonna get this bridle on her, saddle, too, and you gonna ride her."

At two years of age, she was already an athlete, and I needed a horse. I'd been riding quarter horses for the manager of a nearby barn. I had always ridden other people's horses, never having the income or savings to take care of a horse. Now at twenty-nine, I wanted, needed my own. I had gone to Bob a few months before and asked for his help in finding one. His nephew Jerry rode for this barn and told us about the troubled mare. The owners wanted her gone, so the price was right. Jerry brought us a photo, and Bob liked her right away.

When Bob spoke about his old horses, they each had their own story. He'd tell me how one horse was different from the next. How breaking in a young horse requires listening for the slightest clues: a shortened stride trotting to the right, a holding of breath in certain kinds of light, an inability to swallow around loud and fast-moving people. One thing they all had in common, Bob would say, was that they were always trying to get things right. They were totally honest that way, always seeking clarity in the wake of confusion. Like Big Red, the one horse no one could ever fall off. As Bob put it, Big Red would find a way to slide east to west, north to south, and keep whatever body was on top of him upright. Big Red was "damned determined" to keep everyone safe.

"Most people," Bob said one day, "don't think half as much as a horse do."

Looking at the photograph, Bob drew his finger across her topline. "By the looks of it, she's a hell of a horse, and they selling her for next to nothin'."

That was a prerequisite for Bob. You should always get a deal. Never, ever, overspend on a horse. Never.

With no rope or halter on her, Bob soothed the mare's head downward with the stroke of his weathered hands. She softened her tight, upright posture and cocked her left hind leg, resting after a half-hour's worth of grooming. Her long neck and finely shaped head sank to the height of Bob's shoulders. Her eyes blinked as she let free a wide yawn. We could smell the stench of tension trapped inside her clenched jaw. I handed the bridle to Bob, and he struggled to put it in position. Bob's a small, slim man, and not much taller than myself at five feet, seven inches. He lifted his arms above her head and placed the reins over her neck, pulling them up onto her withers. He prepared the bit in his hand. Stretched it between his index finger and his thumb, spreading the broken snaffle wide enough that it could slide through the thin slit between her lips. He moved his hand slowly and played the corner of her mouth with his thumb. Tickling her, she parted her teeth. Once the bit touched the top of her tongue, her head snapped up and she pulled back hard, rushing backward and hitting the stall wall.

"They hurt her. Did somethin' to her mouth," Bob asserted.

The mare's wrinkled butt was pressed up against the wall. Her head soared above us, straining to keep its distance from Bob's hand. He scratched the cowlick that centered itself on the midline of her chest. Little flaky crusts of dried skin scraped off. The mare started to chew and lick. She took a step forward, accompanied by a deep sigh, and balanced herself again on all four feet.

"Never underestimate 'em," Bob said in a whisper, "They sensitive, like hummin' birds." And it seemed the mare heard him, too. She dropped her head, on cue, while Bob raised his hand from her chest to caress her muzzle.

This time he lifted the snaffle up into her mouth, making sure to not touch down on her tongue. He held the crown of the bridle high and placed it over her ears. There were a lot of things to "fix" with this horse. Bob was confident that we could get her through all her troubles. He would teach me how to gentle this mare. How to help her trust humans again. He handed me the reins. I took the left rein, pinched it through my fingers, and closed my palm around the leather. I was three inches from her mouth.

"Hold her loose with those reins," he shouted at me. "She feels every little touch."

Bob pulled the saddle blanket over her back without any trouble. He picked up his precious, dirty saddle and placed it a few inches behind her withers. He cinched it up while the mare stood quietly waiting. I was busy minding the pressure on the reins. Standing off to the left of her, I opened my grip and the rein dangled from the corner of her lip. My own mouth quivered at the thought of riding her.

The manager of the quarter horse barn where I rode told me I was a good natural rider. She picked me out of a group of riders and asked if I wanted more horses to ride. I didn't grow up with horses, like Bob. Every year I would ask for a horse on my birthday and for Christmas. And every year I collected two more plastic horses to put into my growing collection. My fascination for horses came from a place inside me I have never understood. I was told as a child that my deceased grandfather was a lover of horses. That he often preferred to spend more time at the barn, and the bar, than he did with his own son. I never met my grandfather. I never saw a photo of him next to a horse. Maybe the love of horses can skip a generation. Maybe it passed by my father and landed, full saddle, on me. I can count on one hand how many times I was able to ride a horse as a child, yet I'm able to remember the smell, feel, and sight of those horses in full detail.

Most of my youth was spent riding waves along the coast of

New Jersey, or on the basketball court. Bob had forty years on me. I was thinking that I was in over my head. In that instant of doubt, Bob moved back toward me. He took the reins and ordered me to open the door. He stepped through the stall doorway, leading the mare out into the barn alley. She moved light, on her tiptoes it seemed, as I watched from behind.

"Damn, she's somethin'. Ain't she?" Bob shouted in admiration.

The daylight had turned into night. At the end of the barn aisle was a bright, half-lit riding arena, part indoor and part outdoor. Half light, half pitch black. We walked her to the end of the aisle, passing the barn workers on the way.

"What's her name?" I asked them as I walked by. *Belle*, they said politely, looking shocked at the sight of her all saddled, bridled, and ready for a ride.

"Be careful," they said again as we passed.

Bob opened the gate, and we walked out into the sandy, lit end of the arena. It was here that I got my first real look at her. She looked at me, too, under those bright lights, her eyes witnessing every step I took. She was a streamlined locomotive; every inch of her body cried out for speed. I should have been terrified. I should have questioned the whole idea of riding her, but there was something about being with Bob that erased my fears. The way he stood, so still and calm, in front of her. The way he caressed her neck with long, quiet strokes. How rhythmically his chest rose and fell, like he was in a deep, comfortable sleep.

I was standing on her left side, up toward her shoulder. I placed the reins over her neck and then gathered them in my left hand as gently as I could. I began lifting my left leg toward the stirrup when I felt Bob grab ahold of my foot, and with one quick motion, he swung me into the saddle.

"Whatever you do, don't hold her back," was the last thing I heard him say.

I pushed my arms forward, straightened out my elbows, and she rode off at a trot. She gained speed quickly, then rolled up effortlessly into a canter. She was soft underneath me. Her muscles circled under my seat. I could barely feel the touch of ground. All normal concussive forces evaporated, and I floated on fast-moving clouds. Her breath took on a constrained rhythm. It caught halfway in her exhale. I put her up to a faster canter just by thinking. I knew not to touch my legs against her; that kind of contact could make her pitch me. I leaned forward in Bob's creaking old saddle, closing just the uppermost part of my thighs, working for a feel of stability. I moved the reins into my right hand, shoved them forward up her neck to make sure not to draw contact with her mouth. I grabbed the back of the saddle with my left hand, just in case she went into a buck. She went out around the outer rail of the arena, which was over 300 feet long. As we gained speed, I heard the thump of her four-beat gallop hustle up underneath her. *Ta dunt, ta dunt, ta dunt, ta da.* Soon we were out into the night. I was blinded by the transition from lit indoor arena into the dark, and the only thing to do was trust her sight.

Riding on young, troubled flesh, the curl of her stride coming up underneath me, pushing upward then falling back. Every ten feet the rise of her beneath me returning. Lap after lap, my body fell into her rhythm. Back into the light I saw Bob, his mouth moving, but it was many moments later when I heard him say, "Let her do the work." I leaned forward. Let go of the saddle with my left hand and lifted over her neck. Ready for more speed, she spilled us around the light, then back into darkness. We were animals, left to our own senses, running into the cold black night as if there were no fences. Like we could run through the night and disappear.

"LET'S SIT DOWN and talk about it." Glenda, my lover, didn't want a horse. She was certain she could talk me out of this decision. She sat on the edge of the sofa cushions and patted the space next to her. What could I say to her that would make a difference? That I was trying to save me, save us? We'd been together almost three years, the longest relationship I'd ever had. At twenty-nine years old, I still could not stay committed. In the past, I tore through lovers, at times dating three people at once. I was already close to having an affair, even looking for my own apartment.

"Why a horse? We can't take on a horse. Where would we keep it?" she asked.

Glenda leaned against the back of the couch. She listened as I told her the plan. How Bob was going to help me. How we had already met Belle, and I had ridden her. How we had prepared the barn and were ready to drive to Charlotte and pick her up.

"I'm getting a horse." I sat straight up on the couch. Glenda stared back at me, her eyebrows compressed and furrowed with frustration. She took a long, deep breath and moved a few inches away.

I could hear the washer whirling our clothes around on the final spin. The earthy scent of beets cooking on low boil swelled from the kitchen. They were close to being soft enough to remove from the stove. I rose from the couch and stepped toward the kitchen.

When we moved into this cabin together, I fought every decision we made for our new home. Buying a refrigerator, a washer and dryer—these felt like a cage around me. I thought I was fighting for my freedom. Instead, I was running backward toward the one place I knew: the loneliness of my childhood.

Glenda walked up behind me as I poured cold water on the beets and started to peel the thick, black, purple skin away from their bodies. She wrapped her arms around me and pressed her waist up to mine. The beets were hot, too hot to mess with, but I kept picking at their skins until she let go.

"You feel so cold," she told me and left the kitchen.

I looked down at my purple-blue stained fingers. My nails bitten down to the quick, the cuticles picked apart, dried scabs in their corners. They were the stubby, torn edges of me. When I was younger, I could calm myself down by typing my fingers against my thighs, spelling out the words that raced around in my head. Standing at the free-throw line during basketball games, waiting for the referee to hand me the ball, I typed I N T H E H O L E. I N T H E H O L E. My personal code for HELP.

I rolled the skinless beets around in my palm. Their small ball-shaped bodies looked full of life, full of blood. The stain of something solid and eternal.

My body felt like an empty shell holding them. It held a deadness I had felt since childhood. I had no tether, no cord that tied me to anything or anyone. My stepmother told me, at my father's funeral, that I was the only child my father had continued to worry about. I imagined him up at night, trying to picture where I was and what I was doing. His lost girl.

Riding Belle, I had felt my body thicken. Waves of flesh grew on flesh. From the rise and fall of her underneath me, from the sweat and the squeezing of my upper thighs against her ribs—she hinged the broken parts of me back together. Riding her, I became an earthly thing, a body full and weighted, something that belonged.

I put the beets in a green ceramic bowl, covered them with aluminum foil, and placed them in the refrigerator.

Glenda went back to her computer. I went into my room and shut the door. I took off my dirty day clothes and lay on the bed naked, feeling my body from my thighs up to my abdomen. Fingers rippled across muscle. I felt the bony protrusions of hips and ribs, the long oval cords of quadriceps tighten and bulge on contraction. The ropelike lines of abdominal muscles encasing my torso, holding my soft insides safe.

I rolled over on my side and stared out the double-hung window of the old cabin. I could hear the squeaking of the azalea branches rubbing against the windowpane. "You're so cold," Glenda had said. I shivered and pulled the blanket over me.

NEITHER OF MY PARENTS knew what to do about my extreme childhood shyness, an introversion that kept me from speaking until the age of six. I was a half-girl, half-boy—a genderless thing—in a world that seemed so intensely defined by gender. I knew I wasn't like my mother, nor like any of my three sisters. And yet I was not a boy. I would stand in front of the bathroom mirror, door locked, checking my skin closely for facial hair, for my vagina to sprout a penis. Once, in a fit of enthusiasm, I announced to my entire family, and to my mother's youngest brother Charlie, that I couldn't wait to grow a mustache and chest hair just like him. My mother stared at my father and whispered something into his ear. My father, who had always encouraged my tomboy nature, sank in embarrassment.

I slipped between the cracks of what people were supposed

to be and hid there. Playing sports gave my boy muscles a place
to grow. It felt like the harder I played, the better the chance for
boyhood to emerge. As I grew older, the basketball court was the
only place I felt whole. Alone, but whole nonetheless.

When I was a freshman in high school, I was accepted into a
two-week, all-star basketball camp for girls. It must have cost my
waitress mother and electrician father a fortune, but they managed to come up with the fee. Perhaps my parents hoped that
sending me to this camp could help me become, at least in part,
a socially normal child. They cut into their meager bank account
to make the trip happen. I was fifteen years old.

Carla was also fifteen, on scholarship along with her twin sister, Joan. They had been at the camp since early June, playing
with the college-level players, and they were both good.

"You're from Mainland," she told me when I first met her.

"How did you know that?" I asked.

"Saw your photo in the paper. Freshman starter on the varsity
team. Big Shit," she said.

She had her shorts pulled halfway down her butt, hanging so
low they covered her knees. As she walked beside me, her upper
torso waved side to side, while her lower lip curled around her
upper. *She is so cool*, I thought, then stared back at the ground and
shuffled my sneakers along.

"What team are you on?" Carla asked me.

"Old Dominion," I answered, and she shrugged.

She was on the "Duke" squad. Duke and Old Dominion were
not in the same division. That meant we wouldn't meet up on
the court anytime soon.

"Pickups are at night. You coming?" she asked.

Nighttime pickups were the one time during the day we could

hook up with other players outside the divisions and play more run-and-gun. I told her I would try.

Carla was from Ventnor. She was a freshman starter herself, along with her twin sister. Her high school was only twenty minutes from my hometown, but they weren't in my district. I watched her almost-dreadlocked curls swirl around her ears. She was short, and I knew that meant agile. She walked that cocky jock walk I would later try to imitate: head and neck bobbing back and forth like a turkey's, legs swinging in slow rhythm with a bounce at the end of each stride. Her shoulders rolled forward and swung in time with her prancing legs, as her arms dangled like ropes by her sides.

Later that night in the pickup game, Carla called out, "I got her." She bent down and touched my right hip with her left hand and pushed me back a step. She kept her hand there longer than the referee should have allowed. It laid right on top of my underwear line, which she plucked and sprung as I dribbled up the court. I lowered my stance and put my left arm out to defend the ball. Once across half court, players were screaming and waving for an open pass. Good players—players I would later see coaching in the WNBA. I widened my stance and turned my shoulders away from Carla, bumping back into her pressure with my almost nonexistent weight. I took a jab with my right foot, gesturing like I was cutting in that direction. Carla fell for it. I crossed the ball behind my back and shook loose of Carla. Free of her, I headed down the center lane only to be picked up by a six-foot-two girl I had met in the New Jersey state tournament that spring. I pulled up in front of her and did a double pump fake. Her enormous frame rose above me into the air. I bounce passed around her to the girl she left in the lane, wide open and unguarded. Layup. I whipped around and headed back on defense.

"Yum," Carla said as she came up from behind and tugged my shirttail.

"Carla, leave her alone," a black-haired girl scolded as she ran past me with #22 on her jersey.

"Who's got twenty-two?" one of my teammates barked.

"You, new girl, get her," another yelled.

Twenty-two was Joan, Carla's twin. She dribbled so low to the ground, the ball almost didn't bounce. She had the kind of arms that had a natural hook, like a ball was always meant to be in her grasp. She covered the court like a low-sliding animal. I crouched as low and wide as I could and touched the back of her waist with my right hip bone. She never turned square to the basket, never really looked at her teammates. She saw them all from just over her protected shoulder, the ball skimming across the asphalt.

I didn't like the feel of her control. I bumped against her as she dribbled toward the right-hand corner baseline. Shoving her out and cutting off the driving lane with the jab of my pointy hips. I could see the corner of Joan's lip curl slightly and turn into a smile, when she tossed the ball high into the air, never looking at anyone, over to the six-foot-two-inch girl, who came as close to dunking a basketball as I'd ever seen a girl able to do. I turned and jogged back on offense, my skinny legs tingling under my shorts.

Later that night, Carla and Joan came to my room. We all had roommates, but mine had not arrived back from their games yet. Joan sat on the bed across from us. Carla sat so close to me, the damp skin on our legs stuck and peeled off each other's intermittently. Carla joked about my underwear line. How she could see the bumpy edge of it through my gym shorts. How it distracted her. My face went hot as I stared down at the floor. Joan told her to cut it out.

"She's a flirt," Joan said. "Watch out for her."

A flirt. She said it like it was normal. Like girls could flirt with girls. I remembered the feeling of my hip bones pushing against Joan's back, as we jockeyed for who would be in control. I lost. And now I remembered how that didn't bother me. How, after the near dunk, it felt like I was the player who scored.

Carla came to my room by herself on the last night of my stay at camp. I had just showered and dressed, sitting on the corner of my bed, tying my sneakers, when she walked in. Her face was gentle and calm. It wasn't her clowning-around face, the one with the mischievous grin.

She sat down close to me. This time she threw her left leg over my right and laid it there, swinging. She took my hand and interwove her fingers between mine. Her thumb caressed the softness of my inner palm. No one had ever touched me like this.

The gesture was so sweet and effortless, I could feel my blood pulsing through my veins. I felt pounding around my temples. When she turned to me and headed for my lips, I pushed into her like an abducted child running back toward her lost family. Lips met. Necks, breasts, hips were sucked. I was no longer the girl alone. The girl who would shoot and dribble, shoot and dribble— for hours, for days—isolated in herself in her backyard court. The girl who stuffed tampons, lengthwise, into her underwear, staring into the mirror, wondering when she would become a boy. The girl who, up until now, had been invisible.

DURING THAT SCHOOL YEAR, after we met, Carla and I would travel to our two different towns and spend the weekends together. In between our visits we wrote letters. I kept them in the top drawer of my dresser, beneath my socks and underwear. We never spoke to anyone about our relationship, not having the words or experience to know what to call it.

During one of my visits to Carla's, we went to the kitchen to have lunch. Her mom came in and asked if I would please sit down.

"Ginger, your mother called me last week," she said as she pulled up a chair next to me. "She said she found some letters that Carla wrote you, hidden in a dresser drawer. She wanted me to know about your relationship. She's worried about you."

I slumped in my chair. Carla walked over and sat close to me.

I had always known something was wrong with me. Since early childhood I knew to hide, to sneak away, to keep the truth of who I was out of sight. My mother was worried about me, and I knew why. This thing that I was should never be seen. It was a disgusting thing. And now it was out. I had brought it into the daylight, for everyone to see. Carla seemed proud of who she was. She rarely hid her feelings. Her mother seemed confused about my mother's concerns.

"I told your mother that you and Carla will be fine. That there's nothing for your mother to worry about."

Carla's mom stood up and pulled two plates from the cabinet. She put one grilled-cheese sandwich on each plate, grabbed two napkins and placed the sandwiches in front of us. I watched as she walked back to the stove, turned the grill off, and took the pan over to the kitchen sink. Everything seemed normal, everything except my body, which began to shake.

Carla's mom came over and rested her hands on my shoulders. "Don't you worry," she said. "I'll call your mom again and let her know. Everything is going to be alright. You girls enjoy your lunch." And with that she went down the hallway leading to her bedroom and never spoke of it again.

Carla reached for my hand, but I pulled away from her. A burning knot rose in my throat. I started rocking in my chair. My senses severed. I couldn't feel Carla's body close to mine. I couldn't hear her words or smell the scent of her skin. Trembling, I moved my chair away.

I didn't speak to my mother about those letters for eight years. I learned to hide, to become invisible again. I learned to lie. I spoke to no one about my life, and no one asked me questions. I moved far away from home. I slept around with many women, some of them angry, confused, and sometimes violent. My body, their bodies, our sexuality was something to be ashamed of, to abuse not love. What started out beautiful with Carla became a dark weapon I learned to wield against myself.

Eight years later, when I finally spoke with my mother about those letters, she leaned across the kitchen table, took my hand, and began to cry. She told me she couldn't bear to see me go through what her brother had to endure. My mother has a younger brother who is gay. Like me, he circled on the periphery of our family, living a very private life we knew little about. My mother had to witness her younger brother repeatedly ridiculed and humiliated by a member of her own family. Wiping her tears, she recalled how painful it was to see her brother treated in this way, and she worried that one day I would experience this same hateful behavior.

LEARNING TO WALK

April / 2013

As she walks toward me, I see that most of her weight lists off to one side. Her head cocks sideways. She is definitely crooked. Everything from her waist down looks out of joint. Years of abuse run rivers of pain into her body. Yet Sarah always appears happy. Her rosy-red cheeks, her red lipstick, a Magic Marker around her smile. This natural enthusiasm seems to annoy some of the other residents, but I can see it also commands a canted sense of respect. Sarah is the oldest person on livestock. Before she began to work as a prostitute at a relative's strip club at the age of thirteen, Sarah lived in the country, on a small ranch. Her memory of her childhood with horses is coated in a pink, dusty haze from her thirty years of drug addiction. Her love for the ranch horses, though, is real. She knew they were in trouble, and it was Sarah's voice on the line when I got the first call.

On my third trip to the ranch, I arrive with a trailer full of
horses I have trained. The residents meet me at the main gate,
mouths agape, not accustomed to seeing a woman drive such a
big rig. I drive north up the ranch road, past the pastures on my
left, and pull off under the shade of cottonwood trees, which run
the length of the nighttime corrals. I asked Flor and Sarah to
leave the ranch horses in their pens this morning. If we were to
let them loose, they would certainly attack my horses, and today
we need calm. We unload my horses and tie them to the trailer.
They stand peaceful in the cool, April morning air.

As I tie the last horse, I feel dizzy. I've been holding my breath.
The tips of my toes and fingers are numb. I have that shaky,
fragile feeling. My heart is beating too fast. I can feel it push my
shirt away from my chest. I lean up against my gray gelding Izzy,
who is standing at the far end of the trailer, and lay myself over
his midbody, with my arms draped over his back. Today, for the
first time, I'll be working with all eight members of the livestock
team—six men, plus Flor and Sarah—and I'm nervous. It's not
just that they are all beginners, people who know almost nothing
about horses. It's not just that teaching eight people at a time is an
almost impossible task. Mostly I worry about what to do with the
broken parts: their lack of attention span, their wounded bodies,
their anger, the dullness in their eyes.

I watch the men move about the corrals, picking up manure
with rusted shovels, the handles of which have been broken off.
Bent over and mindless, they roam the corrals like trolls. Their
hoodies cover their rounded shapes. The light touch of sunlight
on their backs seems misplaced.

Alive but dead, I think to myself and begin to realize why I'm so
nervous. Their broken parts look like me. For many years I had
no compass. My ability to perceive what was healthy and good

for myself had fallen silent. No gesture was big or loud enough to wake me. I moved through my days just like these men. Facing the ground. Shuffling my boots. Hiding from myself and everyone around me.

Izzy twists his neck around my slumping body. He puts the edge of his lips on the corner of my jacket and starts to nibble. I look up and see the men hauling the last wheelbarrow of manure out of the corrals. Sarah and Flor are leaning against the cottonwood tree, wearing new cowboy boots and leather gloves. They wave for me to come over. Flor has her long, light brown hair pulled away from her face this morning. She tilts her head to the left and asks if I'm alright. I look again at the men. As they walk toward the hay barn, they remove their hooded sweatshirts. The shape of their torsos looks straighter, more refined. But still, their heads dangle downward from their necks.

"I have a simple plan for today," I tell Flor and Sarah. "I hope it works." I call the men over and ask everyone to gather around me.

"Before we get started," I say, "I want everyone to line up facing down the road." The men strut over in short choppy steps, looking confused and tired. To a painter's eye, it would be a cacophony of forms. Some round, some thin, slumping shoulders, and a few arrogant chests. They hold their heads slightly turned, twisted, and fallen—the shape of defiance compromised by uncertainty.

"Today we're going to learn to walk," I say. The men shake their heads and start to mutter to each other. I line up next to Sarah and ask everyone to watch me. I walk down the road, taking long, smooth strides, my head upright, eyes forward, arms loose and swinging. I turn and walk back, demonstrating the same flow.

"Seems easy enough, so who wants to try?" I ask. No one

speaks up but Sarah, who waves her hand in the air like a third grader.

Under his breath, Tony gives a hiss and rolls his eyes, stares back at the ground. Marcus, the young man who is close to being released from his prison term and beginning his work out, is thoroughly bored. He's yawning and staring off at nothing. With one hand on his left hip, his weight shifts onto his right leg. He has the look of a lone bull in pasture.

Sarah steps in front of me and tries to balance on her twisted frame, both feet spread to the width of her shoulders. She takes her first few steps and veers off to the right. Wobbling down the driveway, trying to correct her trajectory. Each step met with a head, neck, and shoulder bob, as if her entire upper body is guided by one melded muscle. She turns, loaded with a grin, and teeters back into the line.

"This was a good effort," I tell her. "But, please, I'd like to help you?" As I reach my hand out to Sarah, some of the men begin to chuckle. Rex and Paul begin to shove at each other. They furrow their eyebrows, trying hard to look tough. It sends all the wrinkles on their faces downhill.

"If you want these horses to respect you, you'll have to respect yourself," I say, speaking loud enough to command their attention. "How you walk, how you hold your posture, this will tell the horses whether to stomp you or follow you. It also tells them whether you are trustworthy or a fake. Believe me when I tell you, they know the difference." All the men look straight at me, adjusting their bodies trying to find the perfect pose. I watch them fix themselves into false positions, looking back and forth at each other, wondering who's got it right.

I reach out for Sarah again, and gently place my hands on her head, neck, and shoulders, trying to help her find some balance.

I pull down on her left arm until her left hand is level with her right. I stand in front of her, scanning her body for equilibrium. I speak again so everyone can hear.

"Sarah, you love these horses, but you walk around them like a hobbled woman. When they see this, they'll walk all over you. We need to fix this, okay?"

With her head momentarily unified with her body, she concedes with another giant smile. She readies herself again, in front of the line, and steps out. Conscious to correct everything to the left. It's another good effort, and I can see she is proud. Flor greets her return with a high five.

Omar steps forward; Flor, too. They take off together, looking crisp. Their arms swing equal distance, forward and back. The rhythm of their strides so effortless you can hear their pant legs swoosh. Omar's eyes are soft and round like river pebbles. I see stories in them as he comes over and shakes my hand.

"You know, Miss Ginger, I almost finished high school with honors. I played baseball and ran track, too, before I got hooked on meth and started dealing. You think I'll be good with the horses?" he asks. Omar is the youngest person on livestock, his innocence still as intact as it can be after what he's experienced. I reassure him that he will do well.

"Dude, what the fuck? It's just a fucking walk up the road. Get back in line," Randy commands. He has his arms spread away from his torso like he's getting ready to hit something. Before anyone else says anything, I jump in.

"Each of you will need to stay conscious of all your behaviors and movements around the horses. That kind of emotional and physical control is the only way these horses will ever take an interest in you. I'm telling you this; you will have to change, on the inside and out, for this to work. Every person here needs practice. Flor and Omar, that was great. Who wants to go next?"

Randy stomps forward. "I'll go."

He turns and pounds up the road, mad as hell. His head held high, eyes poking out of their sockets. His hands clench into fists. Randy weighs more than 250 pounds and stands about six foot three. It looks like his wife was right to send him here to get control of his anger.

"These horses don't mess with me. I'm not scared of 'em," Randy announces as he struts back into the lineup. Shoulders slouched forward, arms doing a downward punch, popping up and down off his toes. "I know horses. I used to work with them on the track in Florida. I ain't afraid of these ponies."

I look over at the other men who are all shaking their heads.

"Oh," I say. "Well, good. Then why don't you head over to the trailer and untie Billy. She's part Thoroughbred. Second one from the right, with two white socks. Untie her, then bring her over."

Randy's eyes squeeze shut in a long blink. When they open again, he's batting them side to side.

"You want me to do what?" he asks.

I repeat myself as he shuffles his feet and looks at the ground. He gives his head a good shake and the shimmy of it travels down his baggy jeans. A few moments pass as he manages to put his hammering body back together, leaving for the trailer at a much slower clip. The residents break the line and come behind me in a semicircle. The horses are standing at my trailer, each tied with a chain of slip knots and a lock at the end of each one. Randy's first challenge will be to tuck his enormous body between my two biggest horses and release those knots, standing only inches away from Billy's mouth. He stops at the corner of my trailer and points to Moo, my Morgan gelding who's tied at the near end of my trailer.

"This one?" Randy asks.

"No, dude, the next one. What, you can't see the difference?" Tony interrupts. He's been stone quiet so far today. Tony hangs onto control by believing he's the smartest fish in this tank. And he may be, but that doesn't necessarily make him a good man. Omar, Paul, and Rex all look away from Tony and back to me.

"You want some help, Randy?" I've been holding myself in place, rocking my body back and forth, trying to suppress my desire to run in there and rescue him.

"You want me to go in there, untie her, and do what?" Randy's shaking a little, his lips no longer pinched tight but held apart and panting. "There's no way I can go in there, Miss Ginger, no way," he confesses.

I walk over to the trailer with all the residents coming behind.

"Everyone likes to say that we can't show our horses any fear, but I disagree. What they need most is honesty. If you are truly honest about how you feel, your body will show it. The horses know the difference. You've got to let that fear leave your body, Randy. Slow down, take a breath. You can do this."

Randy steps into the thin space between the two horses, cursing "fuck this" a few times.

"Lay your hand on her rump, Randy; let her feel you."

Randy lifts his arm above Billy's tall rump and places his open palm on her bronze-brown coat.

"Now, walk up to her head, allowing your hand to travel lightly along her back as you go. That's nice, Randy. Good job." Randy's face hangs loose from its frame. His anger no longer able to cling to the usual bony attachments. I coach him up the lead rope. He unlocks the slip knots, releases each one down the chain. He is quiet now, gaining confidence in the steamy space between the two equine bodies. "Now, back her out. Take your lead rope, face her head, and walk into her chest. Don't be too strong with your hands. Billy doesn't need that."

Billy came to me as a rescue. Aggressive, protective, and skinny. I'll never know her whole story. What I do know is, if you want a fight, she'll meet you there. She's quick to watch and read people. Over the last three years, she's shown me how to be more patient, to listen, and to not be afraid to show my weakness. She has stripped me of my false pride. Billy is an amazing athlete, and she's troubled. This combination demands complete honesty.

Billy looks straight back at Randy, like a soldier to a sergeant. Her eyes stick to his face. Her hind legs ready themselves and shift back, as Randy takes his first step toward the middle of her chest. Together they pull out and away from the trailer, with Randy taking long deliberate strides, sweat pouring off his forehead.

All the men, minus Tony, huddle around Randy and Billy as they clear the trailer. Slapping him hard on his back. "Good job, Randy." Rex starts scratching Billy's forehead. "She is beautiful, isn't she?"

Randy hands me the lead rope and bends over at the waist, hands on his knees, breathing heavy.

"I gotta sit down, man. I think I'm gonna faint."

Marcus and Rex grab Randy under his shoulders and hold him up. They scoot him over to the edge of the road, next to a small irrigation ditch, and sit his weakened body down. I walk behind Randy, still holding Billy, and lay my left hand on his shoulder. I want to tell him how proud I am, but I hold back. Instead I stand in silence, behind him, watching his breath labor up and down.

Rex, Marcus, and Paul have come alive and want my attention. They walk up the road together, each with their own unique style of ease, effort, and expression. They want to touch the horses like Randy has, and they'll do whatever it takes to get that chance. All three of these men are athletes. Their ripped stomachs peek out from the thin space between their shirt hems and jeans. All have biceps rounding beneath their sweatshirts, the hidden shapes looking like overinflated tennis balls. Rex, the tallest, could be a runner. Paul, a football player. Marcus, soccer. Sober and clean for a year or two, their eyes sparkle white around intent pupils.

Marcus walks up the road like he is gliding on air. He no longer looks like the tight body builder I met on my first visit. His body swings loosely, like a sailor who's been off to sea for months. His hips undulate like waves. His torso rocks on top of that surface.

"You look good today, Marcus," I tell him. "I don't know what has changed, but you look very relaxed."

"I start my work out tomorrow, Miss Ginger," he smiles and tells me. "I have a few interviews already lined up."

"Oh, Marcus, that's great. I'm so happy for you. I'll get you my phone number. Please, let's stay in touch," I tell him.

Paul holds out his wrist on his return. He wants me to look it over, see if it has healed enough to work with the horses today. Two weeks ago, when Hawk mauled Paul during the evening feeding routine, he knocked Paul down in front of one of the big cottonwood trees and then went about eating his hay. Paul caught his fall with his right hand. He's lucky he didn't break that wrist. Today, it's still a little swollen around the joints, but he no longer needs to wear the wrist brace the doctor gave him. I hand Billy's lead rope to Rex and ask Paul to put his right hand in mine.

"Gather around, you guys. I want to show you something." I walk Paul over to the center of the group, still holding his hand.

"Paul, will you take me for a walk, please? I'll be the horse, and you're the trainer. How will you ask me to come along?" With his good hand, Paul squeezes hard around my palm and pulls me forward. I resist. My arm strings out in front of me. Paul's pulling and laughing. My legs are fence posts pounded in the ground three feet deep.

Being a fourth-generation prisoner, Paul's not accustomed to subtlety. He walks like a gangster, with his shoulders rolled forward from his thick neck. His hands are the size of plates. Arms as wide as my thighs. I watch his legs waddle up the road, like a body builder on steroids.

"Don't pull on me. Give me a signal, something that tells me you're getting ready to walk. You know, give me a gesture."

Paul leans forward from his waist, taking my hand in a lighter hold, and presents himself as a partner would, asking me to dance. His skin takes on the texture of a kiss. I follow his suggestion, and we walk up the road. As he walks, I can feel every hesitant, self-conscious step. It is strange to feel such doubt in a man who has had to be so strong to survive. I reflect back to him his own uncertainties by pausing momentarily. He stops and gestures again to move us forward. We move, melded together, back to the group.

I stand next to Paul, talking to the other members of livestock. Teaching them about the complexities of communication with horses. How they see, feel, smell everything. I still have Paul's hand. I can't let it go. Our palms wrap so softly, they hold themselves. Buoyant and free, like someone else's childhood.

"Now, Paul, take Billy's lead rope into your hand." He slips away from me as Rex gives Billy over. "Ask her to walk, the same way you asked me." Billy has her head low, resting and waiting for a signal. Paul grips the black lead rope and pulls it forward

with one quick jerk. Billy's head swings up and resists. He laughs
at himself again and looks over to me.

"I did too much, I know. I mean, that's . . . that's . . . what we've
been doing, you know, making these horses do stuff instead of asking them. They're pissed at us. We've been too hard on them."

"Bullshit," Tony busts in. "They're fucking out-of-control
monkey shitters. We don't need to treat them like babies."

"Don't start, Tony." Flor takes a stance that shows she has the
power to kick him back to the maintenance crew if he doesn't
shut up. "We're gonna learn a different way. You either get in or
you're out." Tony loads his fists into his pockets and looks away.

"Will the ranch horses ever respect us, Miss Ginger?" Randy
walks up from behind, looking flush and rested.

"If you change, they'll change," I say and motion back to
Paul to try again. This time, he pauses a moment to reflect. He
scratches the cowlick on Billy's forehead; she drops her head. He
leans his torso forward, pushes his leading hand out in front of
her, and begins to take his first step. Billy slides along right next
to him, down the road and back.

Flor steps forward and asks Paul to show her how to work with
Billy. I send Rex, Sarah, and Tony for the other three horses tied
to the trailer. Rex gets Joker, an eight-year-old warmblood gelding. Sarah releases Izzy, my ten-year-old Lusitano. Tony picks
Moo, my fifteen-year-old Morgan. I watch as my horses' ears face
sideways, taking in their new person. I show the residents how to
use the shape of their human bodies as inflection. Go, stop, turn.
They lean forward; they twist sideways; they breathe loud enough
I can hear them. One animal to another.

Rex's long stride is equal with Joker's, who stands almost seventeen hands tall. Both have a bounce and lift to their gait. Izzy is
busy trying to adjust to the new curves of Sarah's body. His ears

twitch in all directions, trying to keep up with her irregularities. Moo is flat-footed, and Tony is, too. Neither of them look at each other. I'm struck by how quickly my horses' personalities have changed to blend with their new person.

"Let's go, Izzy," Sarah sings out in a high-pitch tone. Izzy, who usually drags behind, is automatically enamored with her exuberance. He's walking briskly along, almost trotting, next to Sarah who is heading across the field, skipping and humming a favorite tune.

"I'm fine," I hear Flor yell behind me. Paul's giving her instruction, but she's shutting down. She and Billy haven't taken one step. I walk over, out in front of Flor and Billy, and look into their eyes. Blank. Dull. Gone. I've seen Billy like this before, but not Flor. Trauma pushes everything out of a body. I try to bring them back.

"Flor, what's the color of the comforter on your bed at home?"

She pauses, looks at me, then down toward her shoes. "Blue."

"What's the last meal you remember with your family?"

"Baked chicken. Fry bread. Pintos and green chile in the Crock-Pot. It was my stepdad's birthday."

"Let's take a walk. From your bedroom to the kitchen and sit down to eat a great meal. What do you say?" I take her left hand and send her forward. Billy follows on her right, stride matching stride. When Flor turns back, Billy follows, with her head resting at the height of Flor's waist. On their return Billy takes a deep blow, the mist of it tickling Flor's forearm. She giggles.

Behind her, Tony is having an argument with Moo. He has Moo by the lead rope, grabbing it right under Moo's chin. Moo's neck stretches out three feet, with his front legs planted in front of his head and his back hooves pulled up under his body. He's not moving.

"You are one mother fuckin' stubborn mule. Get your ass up here, you donkey." Tony starts to swing the end of the lead rope. I take off at a run in their direction.

Moo is my most dominant horse. He runs my herd back home. My horses take one look at Moo and walk the other way. No ear pinning, tail swishing, or squealing. Moo eats at whichever trough he wants, he sleeps out in the softest patch of grass and sun whenever he wants, and he claims the run-in shelter when the rain and snow fall hard. No one ever challenges him because he is unquestionably in charge.

I catch the end of the twirling rope from behind Tony. He snaps and turns in my direction.

"This horse is for shit. Why'd you bring something like this over here? We've got enough of this shit already." Omar and Paul run up the road behind me. I stare at Tony as my face feels like it's on fire. I could meet his darkness. I have that in me, too.

Minutes pass. Moo holds his position like a dead-weight tractor. Any minute I expect him to scream. Moo always lets me know when trouble is near.

Only once have I met a creature as messed up as Tony. It was a horse down in Ocala, Florida. A winning Thoroughbred mare who refused to race, who had lashed out violently and injured her jockey and handlers.

I had gone to Florida, in my early thirties, to ride and study with a horse trainer named Danny Martin. Other cowboys told me about Danny, a horse trainer who took on very difficult cases. Sport horses. Expensive horses. Dangerous horses. Horses who had chased off or wounded a half dozen other trainers.

The mare arrived the second day I was at Danny's. She came off the trailer loaded with muscle, stud like. She had a double chain wrapped around her muzzle for control and to keep her from biting us. Danny asked me to put her in his indoor ring. It's an oval-shaped ring about one hundred feet long and seventy feet across. He handed me a leather strap, sewn with fleece on one side. He placed a raincoat in my other hand.

"Put the hobble on her right front leg and get the hell out of there as fast as you can. You'll want that raincoat, too. Believe me."

Hobbles are used to wrap a horse's leg in a bent position, making them bear weight on just three legs. Hobbles are often used in the mountains, in overnight pack trips, so horses can't run away from camp. Danny used them differently. "Most of these horses I get are just looking for trouble. People don't mean a thing to them. If they could, they'd eat us for lunch. I try to find ways they can fight themselves. Then, I leave 'em to it."

Not knowing why, I put on the raincoat and headed into the ring, hobble in my left hand, mare in my right. I picked up her right front leg and bent it back from the knee. Wrapped the leather hobble, fleece side down, around her pastern joint and forearm three times, tight. Unsnapped the chains around her face and ran out the gate. When I turned back to check on her, she exploded. Running wicked on three legs, faster than most four-legged horses I know. As she galloped, she sprayed piss all over me. Whipping her tail and shooting the smelly, thick, yellow urine every few strides. Piss that shot out like pellets against my face, pinging off my raincoat. A kind of piss I'd never seen before, like piss could be used as a weapon. Having one leg completely restrained sent her into a tantrum. I watched her run around the oval like a deranged devil. Her eyes bulged, crackled red lines squiggled across the white. Her body took on the shape of something that only knows hate. Every muscle in her body bulged with rage.

We watched the show for about ten minutes before Danny

said, "Let's get back to work." We left her in misery and started working the other twenty or so horses Danny had in training. Every chance I got, I'd look in on the mare. She was steamy hot with sweat, and vapors that rose off her back. Still trying to trot or gallop away from the total ruin of her forced containment. All day long I could hear the whirl of her inside the ring, scraping against the wooden walls in a crazed frenzy, as troubled as a spinning dog, trying to eat his own tail.

Danny worked us into the evening, horse after horse, until eight o'clock, when his wife called us for dinner. We shared a meal while I sat distracted. I was thinking about the mare and the possibility of leaving her like that all night. As I went to leave, I tried to be casual when I asked Danny if he'd like me to check on the mare in the indoor ring, trying not to appear the emotional woman who cared too much, who wasn't tough enough for this kind of work. He told me that if she was lying down and resting, I could take off the hobble. Otherwise, leave her the way she was.

It was dark in the ring, and I didn't yet know where to find the light switch. But the moon was bright enough that I could make out her shape. She was lying on her side. Her head and neck raised, but the rest of her curled up, like a deer bedded down for the night. Her hobbled right foreleg was facing the ceiling. I unlatched the gate, but she didn't startle. Moving in close, I tried to soothe her with warm tones, ahhh's and ooo's, but mostly they were for me. In case she tried to jump up, I came from behind her, letting her know I was there verbally. Kneeling to her height I stroked her neck, the back of her head, between her ears. All I saw was a serene and resting silhouette. I reached over her back and unbuckled the hobble. She stretched her leg out stiff and leaned back into me, lengthening her neck. She laid her head to the ground while I caressed her whole body. Her hair was matted and whipped dry from all her efforts. Her breath held the rhythm of something that had been ill for some time, but now could finally settle.

TONY'S KNUCKLES ARE turning white from pulling on Moo's face. His hair is fried from the many years of meth addiction. It looks like he's been electrocuted. He has one incisor left on the top of his mouth and two teeth below it. His fat tongue squeezes out around them as he clenches his jaw and leans backward, straining to force Moo to step forward.

"Release the pressure, Tony," I tell him.

"Give me the goddamn rope back," he shouts at me, then jerks the end of the lead rope out of my hand. He wraps the rope twice around his forearm and takes a stronger hold, forcing Moo so far off balance he stumbles forward.

"What the hell is wrong with you. Let go of my horse!"

Moo gathers his hindlegs under and pulls back against the rope. He resets the pressure. He's never giving in. Paul and Omar come closer. Paul stands over six feet tall and must weigh over 230 pounds. He has a tattoo across the back of his neck that reads BACK OFF. Paul, who asked me to dance just moments ago, places both his hands gently on the front of my shoulders, trying to settle me down. He gives me a faint smile.

"We will take care of this, Ginger," he tells me. Each word measured out, slow and exact. "Tony, give that horse to Omar." Paul motions to Omar to go get Moo. Flor, Sarah, and Rex have gathered around us. They stand with their arms at their sides, legs spread, ready to jump in and help if they're needed. No one says a word except Paul.

"Let go of that horse, Tony." Paul has his back to Tony, still holding his hands on my shoulders.

Tony snarls, his upper lip pressed upward exposing his tooth-less gums.

Paul releases me and turns slowly to face Tony. Omar stands in between Moo and Tony with his hand raised, ready to take the lead line. We are all there together staring Tony down. He huffs, jerks his head backward, and makes a gesture with his middle finger.

"Go fuck yourselves," he says, then drops Moo's lead rope to the ground. He kicks the ground with his boot and walks away, heading back toward the men's dorm. Moo lets out one long scream. The vibration of it makes the hairs on my arms stand up.

Omar picks up Moo's lead and walks him back to the trailer. Moo drops his head, licks and chews, with his jaw sliding side-ways around his tongue.

WHEN SARAH FIRST CALLED, she told me how the men were fight-ing with the horses. Pinning them in the corners of the corrals and tying ropes from their halters to their tails to make them submit. She told me how they left Willie, an older black Ara-bian, tied and curled around like this for so long he fell over and couldn't get up. The ranch horses are fighting back. They kick, they bite, and they mean to cause harm. A prey animal turned, by force, into a predator. Men like Tony have punished these horses with their own pain for many years.

I walk toward my trailer, my horses, slow and uncertain. It's time to break for the day. Everyone needs to get cleaned up for dinner, for their GED class, or their parenting class. I load my horses, one by one, into the trailer. Moo goes in last. He stops at the trailer door, refusing to load, and bends his neck around look-ing for something. Then he lets out one last scream.

STRENGTH

June / 2013

Willie was twenty-eight years old when I first met him. A dusting of white frosting sprinkled around his eyes. The rest of his body covered with the far distant color of the night sky. He's lived on this ranch most of his life. There are photographs of him on the walls inside the dining hall, just above the bench.

The founders brought the bench from Ellis Island. It's a long narrow bench that sits facing the entrance to the kitchen. When someone sits on it, no one can speak with them. When the residents first come to the ranch for their interview, they sit on the bench, sometimes for days. Left alone in silence to try and figure out how they got into all this trouble. On Ellis Island, the immigrants sat on this bench waiting for their lives to begin again in a new land. Everything at this ranch is intentional. If you're accepted into the program at the ranch, your journey begins on this bench. If you break any of the rules, the standards of the ranch, you return to the bench and wait for decisions to be made about the severity of your behaviors. To be put on the bench often means you are close to being sent back to prison.

When I arrive each day, I enter the dining hall, walk past the bench, and check in at the front desk. Here I am given a list of names, those residents who should be down at the barn waiting for my instruction. I turn away from the check-in desk and face the bench straight on. The old oak planks of the bench hold a series of concave wells, ancient resting places, where the stain has worn through. Three or four people could easily fit along its straddle. Most days there is someone holding silent on the bench. A lifeless form. No visible sign of breath entering or leaving their body. Almost invisible.

In the photographs above the bench, Willie looks much younger. His midnight-colored, shiny coat throws a polish on his lean and tight musculature. Now he is only a thin shadow of the horse in these photographs. His aged teeth are worn ivory slopes, too smooth to grind. Above his weathered eyes, deep recessed sockets have formed, as if his skull is caving in. Over twenty years ago, Willie was donated to the ranch. All the horses come here as "donations." But there is no such thing as a free horse. Horses are given away because they are difficult, unbroken, contentious, and sometimes dangerous. In one photograph, I see Willie at the back end of a horse trailer, his black silhouette framed by a New Mexican blue sky. His head is high, knees and hocks lifting off the ground, tail arching proudly. In another photograph, a young man is riding him. He sits sloppily in the saddle, with an ill-fitting cowboy hat perched on the top of his head. The reins are gathered tightly around Willie's neck. The rider's hands are gripping, pulling the reins high into his chest. Willie wears a long-shanked, steel bit that extends six inches below his lower lip. The young man looks proud, and proud he should be. Somehow, he got Willie to stop long enough to have this picture taken. Though I have yet to ride him myself, I have been told by older members of the ranch that stopping Willie is a monumental feat. He has run the residents into trees, into corral gates, into fence posts, all in an effort to rub off his rider. There are many stories about Willie. He's an ill-behaved legend.

IT IS THE FIRST Tuesday in June. I'm standing at the check-in desk, talking to Daniel. He wants me to wait for Flor. He says there is something we need to discuss. Daniel is considered an elder here. He's been on the ranch for six years. He and James are the operating officers. They know everything that happens here, on an hourly basis, making endless difficult decisions about each resident. Flor comes from behind and taps on my shoulder, says hello, and takes me by the hand. She leads me over to the bench. There's a shape sitting on the bench, a thick lump of a body: tall, broad, and female.

"Ginger, this is Eliza. Eliza, this is Ginger." Flor tells me that Eliza is the most recent woman to take up residency at the ranch. "Eliza, we're trying to get you off this bench. Sit tight. We'll be right back," Flor tells her. Eliza doesn't look up. She nods her head with the slightest movement.

James and Daniel are standing in front of the check-in desk, and the four of us walk past it, through a narrow, rounded doorway only five feet tall. I follow the three of them, down a hall with a low-arching ceiling, not three feet wide, covered in mud plaster. It's dark and musty with little air circulation. We wind past wooden doorways seemingly made for miniature people. The architecture is almost a hundred years old. Built in the early

1900s from materials found, gathered, and processed on the land around it. It feels like I'm heading to a dungeon.

We make a turn to the right and open the door to our left. Everyone but Flor ducks to get in. The viga-lined ceiling is low, with piñon wood burning in the round kiva fireplace built into one corner of the room. It is early June, and the fragrance of piñon reminds me of the cold winter behind us. The chairs are built like square boxes. The Navajo-designed cushions rest on heavy wooden frames. Daniel asks me to sit down and gets me a glass of water.

"We want to speak with you about Eliza," he says, as he hands me the glass. "We may have to send her back if we can't find another facility more equipped to help her." I don't know what he is talking about, so I sit and listen.

"Eliza's starting to self-mutilate," James informs me. "She's pulling out all the hairs around her face, her scalp, her eyebrows. She's been warned, but she can't seem to stop. She picks and gouges at her fingernails until they bleed. She's despondent and incommunicative. It's getting worse by the day." Daniel bends forward toward me, rests his elbows on his knees, and cups his right hand over his chin.

"We don't take anyone who has a history of suicide. Eliza's records don't mention any mental health issues, but she has old scars on her forearms. She's been here for four months now, and we're starting to worry." Daniel looks toward Flor. "Flor thinks she should join the livestock crew. She thinks maybe the horses could wake Eliza out of her daze. What do you think? Do you have much experience with this?"

I've only been working with the livestock crew for three months. In that time, I've learned I have my limits. My relationship with Tony is still difficult. He's aggressive, he's angry, and he surfaces the worst in me. Outside of these sessions at the ranch, I mostly work with normal people, so-called "healthy" people. People whose biggest problem is choosing what to wear for a lesson and should they cancel in case of rain. Now Flor wants me to work with someone whose tendency is toward self-mutilation. I'm far out of my league.

"I don't have any experience with people like Eliza," I reveal to Daniel. "Where is she from? What's her story?" If I listen to a person's life experience, a horse's background, I usually get hints on how to teach them.

Eliza lived near Albuquerque, James tells me. From an upscale home in a gated community. She's twenty-six and has spent the last five years in prison for drug use and related crimes. She's been to four different rehabilitation facilities. In and out of them since she turned sixteen. Eliza's family was a very successful, drug-dealing family. They worked out of a warehouse in a commercial district, operating as a legitimate business. Eliza worked for the family business since she was old enough to pack boxes, produce shipping labels, and run the computer. By the time she was fourteen, she was keeping the books. The family business was all Eliza ever knew. When she was fifteen, the family got busted, and her parents were sent off to prison. Eliza went to juvenile detention. She's been bouncing back and forth between federal prison and rehab ever since. Eliza's not seen her father or mother in five years, though her father writes her letters from prison—letters she collects but never opens.

Flor is Eliza's mentor. She was assigned to take care of her when Eliza first entered the ranch. The residents who have been here long enough take responsibility for the newcomers. Flor's been here over two years. She's learned how to greet people, to look them in the eye, and to be gracious and thoughtful when spoken to. She's always neat, her hair combed perfectly, and her clothes suitable for a young professional. She has the power to influence Daniel and James's decision, and she's determined to do so.

"I know you both haven't been down to the horses lately, but there are many things we're trying to change." Flor turns in her chair and faces Daniel and James. "The way Ginger is teaching us about the horses and ourselves, it could be good for Eliza."

Both Daniel and James shoot questions at me. "What's the plan? Who will be keeping an eye out for Eliza? How long should we try this before it turns, you know, dangerous? And, Ginger, are you willing to be Eliza's strength if things go badly?"

It is the last question that concerns me.

Flor moves closer to me. "Ginger's already been our strength down there. She's helped me and Sarah. She's helped Randy, Paul, and Omar, too. She'll take care of Eliza."

"I'll be honest," I say. "I don't know how this will go. I've never worked with someone inclined to injure themselves. But I do know a lot about horses, and I trust they'll let me know how Eliza's doing."

"The horses?" James asks. The doubt is obvious in his tone.

"Maybe you guys can come down and watch a little," I say. "It's hard to explain."

Flor and I leave the room together and head back through the hall. Flor hustles ahead of me. I feel sweat bead up and drip down my temples. *Here we go again*, I think to myself. One more person to keep a close eye on. I sigh, then rush forward to catch up with Flor.

When we get back to the bench, Sarah is sitting next to Eliza, her arm wrapped around Eliza's shoulder, waiting for us to finish with Daniel and James. She has her boots and gloves on, ready to go down to the horses. Sarah knows not to go to the corrals alone. The women must always be in groups of two or more when they walk across this ranch. Everyone is watched closely. No flirting is allowed. No touching. If a man or woman gets caught making advances, they are automatically put back on the bench.

"How did it go?" Sarah rises from the bench.

"They said they'll let us give it a try." Flor smiles and gives Sarah a fist bump.

All three of us reach down for Eliza and pull her off the bench.

DOWN AT THE CORRALS, the men are waiting for us. They have Willie, Scout, Estrella, and Hawk groomed and tied to the pipe railing under the cottonwoods. Luna's in her pen. The crack in her face has shrunk over the last few months and her eye is open once again. I asked Paul and Tony to work together and clean Luna's face once a day. I thought it would be good for Tony to learn to take care of someone other than himself. Teaming Tony with Paul gave me confidence that things would go well. They're able to halter her, lead her up to the pipe corral, and groom her. A few weeks ago, we started working with her in the round pen.

I've carried over my farrier tools: new hoof knives, nippers, and a rasp. The horses' hooves are all overgrown. As far as anyone knows, these horses' feet haven't been trimmed in over a year. Scout and Hawk stumble along and frequently trip when we work with them. Estrella has a two-inch crack above her quarters. I haven't felt comfortable working the horses hard with feet this long. Willie is the worst. Being Arab predisposes him to mule or club feet—tall, upright hooves that make him look like he's walking on high-heeled shoes. Willie's the smallest horse we have and, since he's the oldest, I'm hoping he's had some experience getting his feet trimmed.

Randy unties Willie and leads him to the group. Looking around for Eliza, I see she's standing next to Sarah, who still has her arm wrapped around Eliza's back. I ask Omar if he'd like to be the first to try and trim a hoof. Omar's one of the youngest residents at the ranch. He lost his mother to cancer when he was fifteen. He started smoking pot, drinking, and quickly became addicted to meth. When his father remarried within one year of his mother's death, Omar left home and began living on the street. Within a month, he was in juvenile detention for stealing food from Walmart.

Omar approaches Willie, whom Randy is trying to hold still. Willie circles around Randy, already in a panic about the possibility of containment. I show Omar the position he will have to hold so that he can trim Willie's feet. I take the lead line momentarily from Randy, halt Willie in place, and hand Willie back to Randy. I pick up Willie's right front hoof, pull it through my legs from behind, and place it just above my knees. The muscles in my upper thighs squeeze together and hold his hoof in place. Willie starts hopping three-legged around Randy. I hop with him and once he stands still for a moment, I release his leg down. When I look up, Omar's shaking his head.

"No way am I putting Willie's leg that close to, well, you know, between my legs, Miss Ginger," Omar tells me.

"You don't want to try? It's not as dangerous as it looks," I say.

This ranch pushes the residents to try and build skills while they're here. They learn to cook, build cabinets, drive the moving trucks, wait tables, and do engine repair. Saying no to learning something new is not acceptable.

"Once. I'll try it once," Omar concedes.

Omar bends down and picks up Willie's leg. He places it

quickly, right above his knees, and pinches down lightly. Willie rips his leg free with no effort and stands in place next to Randy. I look around for Eliza, remembering I must keep her in my sight. She's in the back of the group now, twirling her hair into thin knots, then tugging on them. Eliza's a large woman, six feet tall and weighs about 185 pounds. With big bones and broad shoulders, she carries the frame of an athlete, with the face of a model.

"Eliza, look up! Have you been watching? Are you paying attention?" I shout at her.

"A little," she whispers, then looks back at the ground.

"Come up here and get closer. Omar, would you mind if Eliza gave it a try?" I ask.

Omar's thrilled he won't have to do it again and resumes his position back inside the group.

Eliza walks forward slowly, dragging her toes across the dirt road as she moves past the others. She reminds me of myself back in grade school, high school, college. Passing through groups of fellow students, trying hard not to be noticed. Her silent, ghost body brushes past Sarah, who takes hold of Eliza's hand and walks her right up next to Willie's shoulder. I hear Sarah repeating herself, over and over, "You can do this, Eliza. You can do this."

Eliza takes her place in the front of the group. Her face holds no expression, a blank white page. *We have to wake her up*, I think, and wonder if anyone ever felt that way about me. I step her through the procedure. Bending down again, I pick up Willie's hoof, put it between my thighs. I close my grip on him for fifteen seconds as he hops around Randy's large body. When I place it back on the ground, I give Willie a good scratch on the neck, and turn my attention to Eliza. She's right behind me, following my every step, though still dull and distant. I make sure she understands everything. The position, holding on with her thighs, being able to take a pull when Willie starts feeling the pressure, and releasing his leg down once he comes to a standstill.

"Are you ready?" I ask her. She tilts her head forward trying to say yes.

I trail behind her, with my hands resting on the back of her hips. She feels wide and solid, like a tree. I put her in position next to Willie's shoulder. When she reaches down to pull Willie's leg through her thighs, Willie's already ahead of her. He throws his leg high into the air and lands it with a great big stomp. Some of the men chuckle, but Eliza doesn't notice the humor. She bends over again and grabs Willie's leg with her thick arms, pulls it through her thighs, and pinches down hard. Willie feels the grab and tries to pull away. Eliza stays with him. Hopping back- ward with Willie as he rears his front legs, trying to run forward and rid himself of her. They take two turns around Randy before Eliza loses her balance, landing face down with a thud. Both Flor and Sarah draw in a worried breath, then run toward her.

"She's got a busted lip," Flor reports. Eliza sits up, covered in dust, a trickle of blue-red drips from her upper lip. I send Omar off for ice.

"We're not going to quit here," I say. "Are we, Eliza? You had him. There is absolutely no reason you can't do this. Now it's a contest. Who's going to win?" I'm down on one knee, looking straight into her eyes, like a wrestling coach screaming, *get up, get up!*

GLENDA ALWAYS REMINDS ME of the day she realized I needed a horse. It was a cold autumn morning in North Carolina. I was riding Belle on the track Bob had mowed for us through his cornfield. The dried stalks crackled and swayed in the wind on either side of us. Belle and I were at a slow lope, just getting warmed up, when a deer shot out of the cornfield and took off ahead of us. Glenda was watching from the hill behind our cabin, which bordered Bob's land.

Belle spooked sideways into the corn at first, then gathered herself and raced after the deer, who was flying ahead at about twenty miles per hour. We were fifteen feet behind her when the doe made a sharp right into the cornfield. Belle crashed through the broken stalks at a full gallop, the corn slapping our faces as we slashed by.

I was in trouble. That morning I couldn't get Belle to open her mouth and take the bit. She was getting more resistant to the metal after every ride. Bob had made a bitless bridle to try, a leather bridle, built just the same as a standard bridle, only the reins attached to a ring underneath her chin. This was our first morning wearing it. With no metal in her mouth there wasn't a way to hold Belle back. When I tried, she pulled against me and started thrashing her head in a tantrum. We were moving so fast there was no way I could jump off. And there was no way to turn her away from the deer. She would have tossed me if I tried.

Through Belle's pointy ears I could see the deer's back end, her white fluffy tail rising and falling in quick succession. I needed to be strong, so I gripped with my thighs. I needed to be smart, so I started to breathe. I needed to trust myself, so I lifted out of the saddle, leaned over Belle's neck, and grabbed her mane.

Glenda says she stood on the hill in shock, watching us chase that deer through the field. She was terrified, mesmerized. It was at that moment, on that particular day, when she finally understood how a horse can save a person. How they can bring a body back to life. I had stopped talking or sharing conversation with Glenda at that time. Withdrawn and depressed, I rarely spent time at our home. When I did come home, I went to my room alone and closed the door. The feeling of Belle's back rounding underneath my seat, the way her ribs expanded and pushed against my calves, the rush of air pumping through her lungs—I could feel my entire nervous system firing under my skin. Watching me hover over Belle's neck, standing up in my stirrups, and latched onto Belle's mane for dear life, Glenda saw something she had not seen in over a year—my body: strong, solid, and alive.

We came out of the field onto Bob's farm road, riding at a lope. The doe in front of us was much calmer, running at ease, accepting us behind her like we were part of the family. Belle slowed her pace, first fifteen feet behind the doe, then twenty. Finally letting the deer run ahead of us, back toward the forest where she belonged.

ELIZA'S EYES ARE open now, their whole circumference visible, no longer hiding behind her droopy lids. With most of the hairs pulled out from around her face, she looks lighter than her size. She doesn't wait for Omar to come with the ice. Back in position, she reaches down for Willie's leg and starts over again. Willie pulls against Eliza's grip and raises both front legs into the air, performing a mini levade, about two feet off the ground. Eliza tucks, squeezes, and performs it with him, moving in tandem off the ground and then back down. Willie bounces off the earth and pulls free of Randy's grasp on the lead line. He's lurching forward on only three legs, free now. Eliza's hair flies forward and covers her face. They circle the barn lot, Eliza leaping back and up, like a kangaroo in reverse. Holding tight to Willie's leg like her life depends on it. Willie comes to a stop right in front of the hay barn. Eliza loosens her grip and Willie's hoof falls to the ground.

She unfolds her torso, stands up straight, and lays her left arm across Willie's back. Flor and I lock eyes.

"You know," Eliza says, "I can tell he wants to be free, but he doesn't seem anxious or mad about this." It's the first full sentence I've heard her speak. Her upper lip now twice as big as her lower. She scratches the line of bug bites bubbling on Willie's chest. He picks his head up and lengthens his neck, pokes his nose to the sky, pushing into her touch. I move toward the hay barn and off to the side of the cottonwood tree. I see Daniel and James watching from inside the tack-room shelter. They sit in the back corner of the shed, on five-gallon buckets turned upside down, hiding themselves from our view.

The lead rope swings from Willie's chin. No one's holding him. He's free to run.

"One more time. Pick his leg up one more time. If he's good, we'll start trimming," I say to Eliza.

Randy walks over to grab the lead rope. "No, leave them alone." My command stops Randy in place.

Eliza turns and positions herself. Willie's ears go backward as he listens for her. For the first time, I realize how quiet it is. The rest of the crew is enthralled by Eliza and Willie's transformation. They watch carefully, creeping in closer to get a good look at the bottom of Willie's hoof. She touches him just behind his knee to pick up his hoof, and he flips it off the ground and lands it in her hand. He lowers his head and doesn't take a step when she presses his leg between her thighs. With his leg between hers, Eliza looks up to find me.

"He's ready, Ginger. I can feel it. Where are those tools?"

Rex carries the tools over to Eliza and Willie. I lean over her back while the rest of the residents gather around us in a tight bunch of bodies. The bottom of Willie's sole is cracked and ready to peel away from his hoof wall. I show Eliza the right-handed hoof knife. It curves into a crescent moon, matching the shape of a hoof. I hang over her, as if I am her arms, and take the knife to Willie's hoof. My palms and forearms face up as I glide the blade over Willie's sole, slicing at dead hoof growth that needs to be trimmed away. His feet are as hard as stone, but the knife rides right through. I have to be careful not to cut myself. As Willie's hoof peels away with ease, I realize I'm getting nervous. I will be handing this blade over to Eliza. Right in front of James and Daniel and all the other residents. Everyone's aware of her struggles.

I take Eliza's hand and wrap it around mine, showing her the movement of our wrists, the pressure of the blade. I smell my breath mingle with hers as our bodies wrap around each other. She, holding my hand. Me, hovering over her like a mother.

It's steamy in our huddle, my shirt sticks to my belly and my back. Eliza's forehead is wet with sweat. It drips down the side of her cheek.

"Ready?" I ask, close to her ear.

"I am."

I turn her right hand over and put the knife in her palm. She holds it lightly, like an egg. I guide her hand sideways from the wrist, showing her again the motion of the blade. As our hands slide together, I see the thin jagged lines across her forearm twist and straighten. Eliza grunts out a breath, trying to hold onto her bent position. We place the blade down on Willie's hoof and begin to carve.

GREEN ACRES

June / 2013

"Ginger, Willie's sinking. He's in the goddamn septic field, and we can't get him out," Tony shouts over the phone. "What do we do? If I try to move him, he starts thrashing around and goes deeper. It's like he's in quicksand."

"Jesus. What the hell? How'd he get in there?"

"They took the fence down yesterday."

"What fence? Shit. How deep?"

"He's in over his belly. You know the fence they had up around the old septic field? They took it down, the stupid fucks."

"For Christ's sake, Tony. Let me think . . . alright . . . alright. Get some alfalfa. Put it down right in front of him. Get him haltered. Keep him still. Give me twenty minutes, and I'll be over."

I train and teach riding lessons at a horse farm two miles north of the ranch. I walk back into the arena, where I have just finished teaching a lesson, and tell my client that I've got to go. I have a lunch break, then two more clients in the afternoon. I'll call and cancel. I've been changing my schedule a lot lately. Trying to fit more time in at the ranch. They still don't pay me for my work, but that doesn't matter. I'd rather spend time around some of the people on livestock than just about anyone else. When I'm with Sarah and Flor, Paul and Omar, I feel more alive than I have in a very long time.

I make my calls, cancel my lessons, and run off looking for the farm manager to tell him I need to borrow one of the farm's tractors and what I'm going to attempt with it. He suggests the small Kubota with the bucket on the front. "Anything bigger might sink," he says.

The black driver's seat is scorching hot. I drive out the gate and turn south onto our poorly maintained county road. The bulleted potholes toss me up and down. I look like a white kernel of popcorn, flying down the road at top speed, 25 miles per hour. The scrappy neighborhood dogs run out to bite my tires. I pass three different burned-out trailers. Meth has been in residency for a long time in this part of northern New Mexico. Two older men on bikes ride up the middle of the road and slow me down. They're heading to the small, family-owned tiendita to buy their minis, the tiny liquor bottles our governor wants to make illegal. I've seen these two men most days when I stop in to get gas. Their saggy pockets stuffed with driblets of alcohol, easier to carry and to drink, as they ride their bikes along. They wave at me with already inebriated faces as I pass them on the left, trying to get the tractor back up to speed. I wonder how long Willie's been sunk in that field.

I drive up to the ranch entrance where Omar and Rex meet me

at the gate. They've been waiting for my arrival. Seeing me on the tractor brings their faces some relief. They pull the gate open and I bounce through the entrance, like a kid on a trampoline. Rex comes over to the tractor and asks what they need to do.

"Run and get as many shovels as you can find," I tell him. He and Omar take off in different directions and return quickly, shovels in hand.

I look to my right and see Tony, waist deep in sewage, standing next to Willie, holding him by a short lead rope.

This ranch sits on a floodplain, and the old septic field, now abandoned for a brand-new wastewater treatment facility, is usually fenced off from the residents and the horses. The fences were removed to start rehabilitating the area, and it didn't take long for Willie to seek out the lush grasses growing out of the fertile soil. The Rio Grande rises in the spring and early summer. Mountain runoff pours west and east along smaller creeks, arroyos, and rivers. The spring flooding affects all the farmland alongside the Rio. River water bubbles to the surface on any low-lying land. The timing was just right—or wrong—when the fence came down. With the old septic field flooding from below, Willie walked right in and dove down for the sweet, young stems.

I wave to Tony. He looks up and then back down at Willie, who is as happy as a bug in juice, eating his alfalfa, standing in the sewage that floats up past his belly. Just beyond the septic field is a line of old cottonwood trees that border and wrap around Swan Lake on the south side of the ranch. The septic field has goo oozing to the surface. Tony and Willie stand in the middle, with the bright green leaves of the ancient trees sparkling behind them in the late morning light. I need to gather myself. I throttle down the tractor.

"We've got to get them out of there as fast as we can. I'll dig till I hit something firm enough they can walk through. You'll have to keep shoveling the shit off the trail as I dig," I tell everyone.

I barely recognize my team. They have their worst set of clothes on for this occasion: torn jeans, dirty, sweat-lined baseball caps. The women have their hair pulled up and stuffed underneath old winter hats, wearing baggy sweatshirts three sizes too big. Their faces are pale, empty, and remote. No one is enthusiastic about walking into this swamp, and for some reason no one is talking. I feel like I've walked in on a married couple at the end of a heated argument. Eye contact is sparse. Rex, Randy, and Omar stand fifteen feet away from Flor, Eliza, and Paul, who stand together in a clump. Saving Willie isn't the only problem they have today, but it's my job to make it their priority. Corralling these difficult personalities into a functional team is the primary goal on this ranch. Even Flor looks caught up in the aftereffect of some turmoil. Her clearheaded confidence has evaporated. Today I can't tell her apart from the cloud of recovering addicts and felons who stand next to her. How easily recovery can be stripped away, I think.

"You want us in front of you or behind?" Omar asks.

"Both. I'll try not to splash this crap all over you," I say. "I have to dump the buckets of this mess somewhere. Where should I put it?" Randy and Rex gesture over to the hard driveway where I'll make the pile.

I fire up the tractor and spin 160 degrees to the right. I give the crew a quick jut from my chin and kick up the hydraulics, grinding the gears into four-wheel drive. I lever the bucket down and dig beneath the soggy grass to pick up my first load. It comes out of the ground like soup. As I pull up and out, the tractor tires spin septic debris into the air. The muck of it lands on the tractor hood, my baseball cap, and the residents all around me who are shoveling fast, trying to keep the sludge from sliding back into my hole. I back up, dump, go forward again, and lunge the tractor bucket into the ground.

My buckets of decomposed poop create a mountain of stench. The livestock team looks sick to their stomachs. They have their sweatshirts pulled up and over their noses. Every so often, I see Randy bend over in a fit of dry heaves. He picks his shovel back up and continues with the mission. The orange tractor looks bruised and incompetent, with dark-brown plops dotting its surface. About four feet down, we hit something hard. *Clack. Clack. Clack.* Round river rocks clank against the steel bucket. It's the old riverbed from before the dams were built, when the river wandered wide through what is now considered the bosque, or river forest. It will hold the tractor, so I move forward onto the new surface and start digging again. We're making some progress.

When I check on Tony and Willie, I see that Willie is unconcerned about the commotion going on around him. He's busy gumming the alfalfa with his ancient teeth. Tony's as quiet as I have ever seen him. He holds Willie's lead in his left hand; his right hand lies against Willie's mane, rubbing the crest of it back and forth.

Tony runs manic most of the time. He talks fast, walks fast, and halters the horses fast. Even when he's standing still, he has moving parts that won't quit. His fingers wiggle up and down, and he pinches his lower lip in such a grip with his one upper tooth that a thin, pitchy breath comes through its crack. He is smart, physically strong, college educated, and was a meth addict for twenty-five years. He pulled off this habit most of his life while holding down demanding jobs in the aeronautics industry. Then one night, he slammed into an oncoming car, totaling the car and injuring all of the occupants. He was sentenced to ten years. Six he did in prison, and then he interviewed to come to this ranch for the remainder. When I met Tony, he had been on the ranch for only six months.

I thrust the bucket back in. Five feet wide, four feet deep, fifteen feet long. Our trail is holding. Two hours have passed and about another fifteen feet to go. We're covered in waste. The smell worsens as we dig. There's no getting used to it. The sun has baked sewage onto our pants, our arms, the inside of our fingernails. We can't wipe the sweat off our faces for fear of smearing muck onto the one clean surface we have. The residents hold to their silence. They're all business. Omar, Rex, and Randy have taken the lead; they shovel the extra sludge away as I back out and continue dumping. Everyone else follows behind me as I reenter the septic field, scraping up the crud that creeps back behind the tractor. All at once I realize Sarah's not with us. I've worked for hours without noticing her absence. I turn down the hydraulics and call to Flor.

"Where's Sarah?"

Everyone in unison shouts back at me, "She's on the bench."

"Is she okay?" I ask.

"Don't know. We're not allowed to talk about it." Flor's answer is quick. She never looks up from her shovel. Here it is, I think to myself. Here is the extra trouble I have felt today, sunk under this pile of floating sewage.

Fuck. I can't lose Sarah. She won't make it back in prison.

I push the throttle up to 2500 rpm and stab the bucket into the earth.

WE'RE NOW FIVE FEET AWAY. Willie and Tony concentrate on the ground. Nothing breaks their focus. Not even this nasty, smoking tractor that spews sludge around as I dig. I take out a few more bucketloads, then put the bucket down and turn off the tractor. I'm a mere three feet in front of them. Omar and Rex take over. Shovel and toss. Shovel and toss. They look like rat terriers going after a ground squirrel. Everyone else leans on their shovels. Still, no one speaks. No one jokes. The day has taken a toll.

Tony starts sucking his leg out of the steady stance he's held for hours.

"Shit, I lost my boot," he says, with one soaked sock stepping onto the path laid out before him. He bends Willie's neck around to show him the direction. *Shhhwappp.* The sound of sludge releasing Willie's hooves pops into the air. Willie stumbles and falls forward onto the clearing. *Clickity. Clickity. Clickity. Clickity.* I hear the knock of his hooves hit the rocks. I turn on the tractor and reverse myself back onto the driveway. Everyone follows. We stand together, waiting for Willie and Tony to make their way. They walk toward us, slipping and sliding on the slimy surface of the river rocks. Willie's head is low, almost touching the ground with his nose. He bends his knees and crawls out, like a dog after a thunderstorm. Tony keeps a loop in the lead line, leaving Willie to balance on his own. His one shoeless foot working harder for traction.

We move like a grimy railroad gang as we walk down the drive and turn north on the ranch road heading to the corrals. Tony and Willie walk the pasture edge, just to the left of the road, moving slowly. Tony's sock is pitch black. The hard ground and brittle grasses make him shorten his stride.

Down at the corrals we pull the hose out, put the spray nozzle on, and turn it to *jet*. The water shoots out in a firm, thin stream that knocks the clods of septic debris off our clothing and skin. Tony stands still and patient. He hasn't said much on the return to the barn. It's as if he's been placed in a liquid meditation chamber, floating in water. He seems so completely different. His breathing goes deep and deflates the rigidity he usually carries in his shoulders. They roll forward and down, away from his ears. He has his legs spread just wide enough that he can rest himself, leaning slightly backward. His arms fold across his pooched-out belly. Willie's lead dangles from his thumb.

"How you doing, Tony?" I ask.

"Good. Good," he tells me. His head and body bob up and down as he speaks.

"You want to hose Willie off?"

"Yeah. Oh yeah."

He waits patiently for the last resident to rinse their body clean, then he picks up the hose. He turns the nozzle to *mist* and starts spritzing Willie along his back and loin, rubbing his palm deep into Willie's coat. Willie's springtime, black, shiny hair begins to reappear. Tony drops the lead line and follows the mist around to Willie's other side and scrubs him clean. Once he's finished, he washes himself off and leaves Willie to stand on his own, while he pulls the hose back onto its reel.

"Goooooood boy." He squeegees the water off Willie's back with the edge of his hand and looks over to me. "Thank you for coming today," he says. "You didn't have to come. I mean, I know you ain't making money at this. Daniel and James told me." He pauses, then wipes more water off Willie's chest. "I'm sorry about how I acted with Moo." He looks away from Willie and right into my eyes. "I really was an ass. I hope at some point you can forgive me."

No one has ever apologized to me so candidly and honestly. No one, that I can remember, has ever taken full responsibility for something awful they have done. And I can't remember a time when I have, either. I shouldn't, but I feel uncomfortable with this much clarity, this much sincerity. It makes me look in the mirror, and I'm not liking what I see.

"I'm sorry, too, Tony. For my anger. For not finding a better way to speak to you."

Again, he looks right at me, but I can't meet his gaze. I shuffle my clean, wet boots in the dirt and the dust sticks, turning them a dark brown.

"Why do you come over here? Why keep coming? Is it Luna?"

"It's not just Luna," I confess. "I come because I need to, because I want to. It's helping me, too."

Tony takes his arm, wraps it around my shoulders, and gives me half a hug. "That's cool," he says and smiles the first true smile I have ever seen grace his face.

I feel relief to just admit it. I come because I need to. Because it helps me. Because I want to. Because it feels like home.

"Are we finished for today, Ginger?" Flor comes up from behind. Her baggy clothes are covered in green-brown smears and still she can't meet my eye.

"Are you alright, Flor?" I ask her.

"Yeah," then a long pause. "I'm just tired," she tells me. I remember one of the first things Flor ever told me about herself, that she's a compulsive liar. It is something I think about often when I am around her. On the outside she is a perfect role model. Her clothes, her hair, her manner of speech—these outward manifestations draw a portrait of someone on the road to recovery. Yet I can't help but wonder what she feels like on the inside. Would she even be able to say?

Everyone looks dog-tired and hungry. It's dinnertime.

"You guys go ahead to your dorms and get cleaned up. I'll see you in the dining hall," I tell the group.

I look up the road toward the dining hall and see Marcus walking down to the corrals. I haven't seen him since he started his work out. He gives me the happiest wave I've seen in months, then rushes over for a hug.

"I got a full-time job today," he tells me after a long embrace. "I'll be working for a trucking company, making seventeen bucks an hour."

"Oh, Marcus. That's exciting. Please stay in touch and let me know how you are doing."

"I will, Miss Ginger. I will." He walks over to another group of residents to tell them the good news.

I hang back with Tony and Willie. Tony is taking his time combing Willie's mane and tail. He doesn't seem in a hurry to go anywhere.

"Tony, are you ready to put Willie back in his corral and head to dinner?" I ask him.

"You know, Ginger, I haven't felt this good in a long time. I'm forty-five years old, and I'm just learning to give a damn. You know, to care about others. Willie let me do that; he trusted me. I mean, it felt good to have him trust me. No one trusts me. Never have. Guess I've never earned it, either, now that I think about it." Tony stares past me as he speaks.

He pushes slack into the lead line and gestures for Willie to take a step. Willie's weathered eyes are half ovals. He rolls them backward in their sockets and yawns.

"Come on, Willie; let's get some rest."

TONY LEAVES ME at his dorm room, where he can shower and get into a clean pair of clothes. My clothes are wet and still stinky, but I enter the dining hall anyway. The residents are just sitting down for dinner, and I feel like a grotesque sideshow distraction. I come through the doorway and turn right toward the check-in desk. Turning right again, I stop at the bench where Sarah sits. Her head tilts sideways. Her bottom lip sags and I can see her tongue pressed up against her bottom teeth. She lets out a sigh with each exhaled breath. When she looks at me, she looks confused, like she can't remember who I am.

I know to follow the rules; I cannot speak with anyone while they're on the bench. I bend my knees and sit down beside Sarah. I feel the stiffness of my back and the ache in my neck from the ricochet of the tractor. I lean my torso against her side and pick up her hand. It is cold, dry, and shaking. Today the wrinkles around her eyes curve down. Her cheery, positive outlook is gone. I imagine this is her prison face, the one she had to wear to survive. I stop myself from thinking about what will happen if she goes back to prison. Instead, I imagine her rose-colored cheeks and lips welcoming me to the ranch the first day I met her.

I look away from her face, down to our knees, which are waving back and forth with worry.

CENTAUR

September / 2013

Paul and Rex are haltering the horses near a pipe corral railing that runs a thirty-foot distance, east to west, and fits neatly between two old cottonwood trees. A large water trough sits at the east end of the railing, a shiny, steel beacon planted right in front of the ancient trees. The horses come here throughout the day to rest and drink in the abundant shade. They huddle together in tight groups to swat off the gnats, flies, and mosquitoes that bite and cling to their chests, ears, and muzzles. To the south of the railing is the bright-green twelve-acre pasture where they spend most of their days, heads down, teeth grinding side to side, ears flicking back and forth.

The horses are all gathered, attentive and perpendicular to the rail, with their lead lines looped loosely around the three-inch metal bar. Each member of the livestock team has a brush in one hand and a curry comb in the other. The sound of horse-hair brushes swooshing across necks and spines whispers into the air.

Tony is standing back from the group, his legs spread wide, hands on his hips. He's upset about something, rocking his torso side to side, trying to contain himself. I ask him, "What's up?"

"Oh, you know, it's Eliza and Randy fighting over Scout again. They're such babies. If they aren't careful, they're gonna get us all in trouble. You watch."

I look past Tony, down to the end of the rail. Randy is on the right side of Scout, combing his mane. Eliza is on his left side combing his tail. They both hold a low-slung pout on their lips. Their shoulders roll forward and down, hunching their backs into the shape of tortoise shells. For some reason, they're both obsessed with Scout, a fourteen-year-old, brown-and-white spotted Tennessee Walking Horse gelding who has his own issues with neurotic and obsessive behaviors.

"They fight over him every day. We're all tired of it. They need to grow up," Tony complains.

Flor comes over and asks, "What's the problem?"

"I'll handle it, Flor," I say to her. "Tony, you're getting too involved. Focus on Luna. She needs your attention. How's her face healing?"

"She's good."

Luna hangs her head low next to Tony's hip. I look down at the scar on her face. It is almost gone. Hair is starting to grow back in patches inside the gray-brown dead tissue, like weeds in the cracks of cement.

"You've done a great job with her, Tony."

"Thank you." He turns his concentration fully on Luna and settles back down.

SOME DAYS the residents are spookily silent, and other days they're full of chatter and chaos. Rarely a day goes by where someone hasn't broken a rule, gotten in a fight, or had an outburst or some other infraction, and that person brings a whole group of other residents down with them. Those troubled days are the silent days. No one wants to talk. They keep to themselves, move slowly around the horses, grooming each horse with steady attention to detail. First the face, down the neck, over the front legs, then back up to the chest. Short, repeated strokes, over and over. They brush the same small corner of their horse's body, like they are staring into a mirror.

As Tony and the others finish their grooming, I give them instructions for the afternoon: what horses they will be working with, the groundwork and riding skills I want each of them to practice. Everyone is listening. They ask questions, then fan out with their horses into the pasture to get to work. Paul works with Willie, trying to get him to stand still for mounting. Paul's big, tranquil body looks like a grounding rod next to Willie's thin, fidgety frame. Eliza bends Scout's neck to the right then to the left. We need his neck to be more flexible, which helps us turn and stop him more easily. Rex is already on Hawk, walking up the road toward the main office complex. Riding Hawk by himself, without another horse by his side, has been a challenge. At times, Hawk still likes to think he's king of the herd and resents leaving the pack. Rex, with his long legs wrapped around Hawk's side, is changing that opinion. Omar and Flor work with Estrella in the middle of the field. Estrella has her saddle on, as they ask her to trot a twenty-foot circle at the end of a long rope.

They each take their turn, standing in the middle of the circle, asking her to keep moving along at the trot. They will warm her up like this until she's settled enough to let them mount. Flor and Omar are proud to say that they are the first people on livestock to ride Estrella.

Tony walks Luna alongside the twelve-foot adobe wall bordering the west side of the ranch. Walking and stopping. Turning and backing. He repeats himself, taking his time. Luna's ears twist and turn trying to listen to each request. If Tony asks too quickly, she'll hit the end of her lead line and try to flee.

Sarah is not with us today. She is still on the ranch, though she has lost the privilege of working with the horses. We don't know if or when Daniel and James will let her back on livestock. I haven't spoken to her in months. She's not allowed to speak with any of us.

Everyone spreads themselves out wide across the twelve-acre pasture, up the road, and over toward the south end of the property, trying to claim what there is so little of here—privacy.

I know they need their space, but I also know that no one is ready to be fully on their own with these horses. If they lose their focus, even for one second, the horses will take advantage of the lapse. These horses remain hypervigilant. We have brought them along from being utterly feral and predatory. They are almost trained, but it is tenuous. They need only one moment, one second of misunderstanding, and they'll launch to assert or defend themselves.

It's called self-preservation, and all horses have it, but these horses have it in spades. Luna is the poster child for self-preservation. She can still be difficult to catch. She lets Tony and Paul groom her, work her in the round pen, and lead her around the ranch. But her muscles still tremble when they touch her. Her eyes still narrow to slits when they approach too quickly. She's stuck in flight mode, always looking for an escape. I was just like her before I met Glenda, before I got my first horse.

Some of these horses may never learn to trust, to fully give themselves over to a human. We must prove ourselves worthy of them. Moment by moment. That's the best we can do. They are the teachers. They keep us present, keen, concentrating.

I make the decision to assign Scout to Eliza today. It pisses Randy off, but he holds it together, standing by the water tank, staring at the ground. Randy, like all the residents, has his demons. A fiery ball of anger pulses just beneath his skin. When he comes close to exploding, he removes himself from the group. He walks over to Willie's gate and grabs hold of it with both arms straight out in front, rocking his body back and forth. His long, sighing exhales make my heart drop to my gut.

"Randy."

"Yeah, Miss Ginger."

"You're working with Moo today. Can you get him from my trailer and take him to the round pen?"

Every day I come to the ranch, I haul Moo over with me. He's my anchor, my horse of choice for anyone who may be struggling. Moo's a solid equine citizen. He will do no harm, and often he helps a resident build confidence.

"Will do, Miss Ginger. Hey, Miss Ginger, did you know? I got the horses up today, all by myself. Groomed them all before anyone else got here."

For whatever reason, Randy makes shit up.

I ignore this lie. He continues, "Where's Moo? Did you bring his saddle? Can I ride today? On Sunday, I worked with Willie, did all the groundwork. Tony helped me. I think I'm ready. Yeah, I'm ready. Think I can ride today? Where's Moo?"

I point at my trailer.

Randy's chatter is the background noise to which we have all become accustomed, a blustery repetition of mostly nonsense. I keep an eye on the residents and horses in the pasture as they work their skills, while Randy fires off his questions and comments without ever looking up or taking a single step. It's as if these verbal calisthenics are his form of a physical activity. Even when I'm fast enough to slide in a few answers to his endless barrage of questions, it doesn't make a difference. Randy doesn't listen.

"I don't know if today's a good day for riding. You still need to get your groundwork skills, and when you get those skills—"

"No, no. I got 'em. I got 'em, Miss Ginger. Wait till you see me. I'm ahead of the game. I can ride. I'm ready. I'm not afraid of these horses."

Randy's world: that's what we call it. As each resident becomes more and more skilled with the horses, Randy lags behind. Everything I teach him is up for reinterpretation. He's a man floating in his own bowl, with minimal awareness of anyone around him. Randy holds onto a fierce denial of his fear around the horses. He is terrified of them. His arrogance and fake bravado repel the other members on livestock. No one trusts him.

He is big but not strong. Hardworking but completely unskilled. Artificially confident, selfish, angry, disruptive, and fundamentally fractured. And he is loud, overweight, and clumsy. He's broad across his shoulders, top-heavy. He waddles instead of walks. He speaks a goofy style of street-gang slang, and he pops up and down off his toes when standing in place, always pumping his arms downward in time with the upward gyration of his legs.

He's a wreck waiting to happen. But he loves, loves, loves the horses. Two months ago, Randy put himself on a diet, proclaiming himself a vegetarian. He knows that his overweight body is an obstacle, a teetering, cumbersome mass that could keep him from being able to mount up and ride.

The only horse I truly feel safe enough to let him work with is Moo. Moo, I know, will not flat-out kill him, which is the fear I hold for Randy whenever he works with the ranch horses.

"Here we go, Moo," Randy scrambles the lead line around his arms.

"Slow down, Randy. Loosen the rope. Be careful not to—" He's not listening.

"Watch out. I got this thing."

"Randy, be careful. You're getting too close to the trailer. Randy!"

"Hey, yeah. Yeah, I got it." He's bouncing up and down in place.

"Randy, listen to me. That's not what I want you to do."

"No, no, no. Wait, wait, wait a minute." He ignores me and goes off on a rant with Moo.

"Dude, listen up. Come over here. I got it. I got it! Cool. See that? Did you see that? Did any of you see that?"

Randy is screaming. His face is flushed. His mouth is wide open and in the shape of a childhood howl.

No one looks his way. No one except Moo. Moo finds Randy absolutely captivating. He is mesmerized by Randy in a way I have rarely seen. Moo, for all his many great attributes, loves to check out from reality. I call him my Dreamer. He likes being gone more than he likes being here. He has a higher calling. When coyotes and bobcats prowl his pasture, when forty-mile-an-hour winds blow his mane and tail sideways, when blizzards white out his entire vision, Moo stands stoic and perfectly still, peering into the portal of a different world. But, with Randy,

Moo is all ears, animated eyes, his hooves adjusting to keep up with Randy's constant jostling motion. Randy is a quirk of nature, and Moo finds him fascinating.

"Miss Ginger, Miss Ginger, Miss Ginger. How 'bout we ride today? I gotta ride today. I'm feeling it."

Why anyone wants to ride horses when they are clearly scared shitless of horses has always interested me. It is fear mixed with a deep yearning, a profound need to be close to the power of an animal. This mixture can ruin a person. Some people make it through, but so many more are left stranded and starving.

Randy's fear is housed in a complete and mindless denial. He can barely handle basic skills, yet he demands I let him ride. Though I have my hesitations, I decide to put my trust in Moo.

"Okay, Randy. If you show me your round-pen work first. If you can perform all the turns with Moo, stop him on cue, back him up, then I'll consider the riding thing. But first you have to prove to me you have the skills."

"I got it. I got it! I'll make you a believer. You'll be singing my praises. Watch me."

As we walk over to the round pen, I watch the rest of the livestock crew work their horses. So far everyone is holding to their focus. From where I am positioned, I can keep them in my periphery while I work with Randy. Working horses all these years has honed my ability to scan for and detect problems quickly.

Randy practices all his round-pen skills in a bizarre but exact sequence. First, he puts Moo inside the circle of the round pen while standing like a post in the center. Then he raises one of his arms out to the side, straight as an arrow, and announces in a booming, affirmative voice, "TROT, MOO." Moo has no idea what Randy is saying, but he reads Randy's body language as clearly as a flashing neon traffic sign. Moo takes off at a trot in the direction of Randy's pointed arrow. Randy stands like a statue with his arm-pointing dramatics and then, out of nowhere, he drops his arm and slaps it rapidly to his side and raises his opposite arm with the precision of a traffic cop. "TURN, MOO." Moo pivots and heads off at a trot in the opposite direction. Back and forth they go, with Randy's long arrows coming up and down, until Randy decides to bring both arms up to his shoulders, then drop them fast and hard to his waist, army style. He tucks his chin to his chest, blows his neck out like a tom turkey, and confidently announces, "HO, MOO." Moo screeches to a halt, their two large male bodies in complete agreement with each other.

The truth is, Moo knows the round-pen work by heart. He has spent years learning all these necessary skills. But Randy's animations make Moo more of a believer. They wake him up out of his dreamy slumber. When Moo isn't asleep, or visiting another world, he prefers to have clear and sharp communication. Mentally, Randy is the definition of uncertainty, but physically he is rock solid. Randy's clamoring, unconscious spewing of the mouth doesn't seem to bother Moo, so long as his physical cues are clear.

Randy goes about backing Moo up at the end of a lead line. Next, he practices moving Moo's shoulders to the right and his hind end to the left. He performs all the turns perfectly. All the while a steady flow of nonsensical conversation floods the air.

"You gotta whip it, Moo. Whip it good. Down to the wire. Like we're on skates. Curl it up. Turn it round. I'm the man. You're the man. Let's get down." Randy is proud. He's doing some awkward stationary dance move. Taking a quarter step out, a quarter step back. He looks like a child who has never learned how to play.

Oh, for Christ's sake, have I lost my mind? This guy has no business sitting on top of a horse.

Randy's giant gestures coupled with Moo's immaculate timing have foiled my plan. I'm reluctant, but I must honor my word. It's time for Randy to get on and try to ride.

Down at the woodshop, Randy has prepared for this day. He's crafted a three-by-three-foot-wide and two-foot-tall mounting box, made from two-by-twelve-inch pine boards, a sturdy platform from which Randy can mount. His vegetarian diet demands he cut out the meat and the fats. He's held to this diet like a religion, losing twenty-five pounds in three months. Each new hole in his belt has brought him closer to riding the horses.

In the tack room of my trailer is the largest saddle I own. I haul it over today and every day, knowing that Randy will eventually ask about it, knowing that someday I will have to allow him a chance to ride. I know Randy's midsection will pour over the pommel and cantle, squish over the skirt, obscuring the saddle. But this is the largest saddle I own.

I take my time and walk Randy through the saddling process. Pull the saddle blanket up and over Moo's withers. Set the saddle down gently on Moo's back. I show Randy how to measure the distance behind Moo's elbow where the cinch will snug up against his ribs.

"Okay, dude, we got the cinch, the horn sits right here, and we got the seat. It looks a little small for my big ass! We're gonna ride; we're gonna ride; we're gonna . . ."

"Knock it off, Randy, and get your shit together. This is a big deal, not fucking playtime. You have to focus!" I feel like a blister ready to pop.

Cinching the saddle on tight, I'm hard and edgy. My throat

burns down the back of my windpipe. I'm holding my breath. Randy's ceaseless talking, his inability to listen, has me reaching for my voice like a knife. I know if I say one more thing, I'm going to slaughter him with words. I clench my jaw and bite down on my lower lip. Moo starts backing away from us on his lead line.

Tony comes back from the pasture, leading Luna alongside. They walk up to the round pen and lean against the top rail.

"Everything alright?" he asks. "Hey, Randy, what's up with the box?"

"I built it for my bigness, what do you think?" He pops up and down. "I think I need it, don't you, to get myself up there?"

"That's cool, dude. Yeah, you'll get up there. Are you getting ready to mount?"

"Not quite yet," I interrupt. "I need to put Moo's bridle on."

I look past Tony. Sarah is walking by with two other women. Randy, Tony, and I turn around to say hello. The other two women greet us, but Sarah doesn't look up. Omar trots over on Estrella.

"Look, Sarah, we're riding Estrella now." She gazes into Estrella's face but ignores Omar. A cold wind seems to whip around her as she turns her stare back to the ground and hurries away. It feels like I've lost a good friend because of an argument I didn't know we had.

"I wish they would let her back on livestock," I tell Randy and Tony. "I don't understand why she can't be back with us."

I turn, pick up the bridle, and move toward Moo. I take three long breaths, spread the bit out between my fingers, lift it up between his parting teeth, and pull the crown of the bridle over Moo's head. I lay the reins over his neck.

Forgive me, Moo. What have I gotten you into?

As Randy climbs onto his handmade box, the platform digs
into four inches of dirt that cradles the sides. Holding the reins
snug and grabbing a piece of Moo's mane in front of the saddle
with his left hand, Randy takes his right hand and twists the stirrup around, where the toe of his left boot can easily slide into
the small square space of the stirrup and help power him up and
onto Moo's back.

Randy has tried to prepare for this moment, more than any
of us could ever imagine. He raises his big brown boot toward
the stirrup and tips it through the center until it touches the side
of Moo's awaiting ribcage. Randy's belt is eye level. I see all the
empty holes he has conquered over the last few months, and yet his
hairy belly still flops over the buckle. The holes in his belt punc-
ture my frustration with Randy, and for the first time today I feel
his tenderness. He thrusts some weight down into the stirrup, getting ready to rise upward. I am standing in front of Moo, the lead
line clutched in my palm, making sure Moo doesn't take a step.

The mounting block quivers in the sand. Randy's legs tremble.
All of a sudden Tony climbs up on the top rail, reaching out
toward Randy with worry written all over his face. I hear a long,
sorrowful note crawl out of Randy's mouth, and I look up to
meet his eye. In that moment he breaks. Water falls downhill. His
torso curls in half. His foot falls free from the stirrup as he folds
and collapses from the mounting box to the ground. The sound
that comes out of him is subterranean, like a beached whale, blow
after blow, deep and lonely. One of his legs lies across the box,
the other folds underneath him. Hunched over and sobbing, his
head slumps forward with his hands cupped over his face. His
wailing sings out into the pastures, and the residents turn toward
us, then run back to the round pen with their horses. They tie
them to the pipe fencing and rush over, staring down at Randy's

crumpled body on the ground. We sink down around him, comforting him. Touching his big, lumpy body like a baby's. I can feel our knees pressing together. The skin of our arms sticking to one another. Randy's sobbing is thick, wet, unstoppable. Our bodies form a capsule around him. We are the blood, the bones that hold him together. Eliza kneels behind him, propping him up. One hand hides the surprise forming on her face, the other rests on Randy's shoulder. She can say nothing without sobbing herself. We are stunned into silence watching Randy's body heave up and down. And then Flor cracks open. Her face hangs hollow. Her eyes fill with tears, then pour over her cheeks. Tony is visibly uncomfortable. He stands up and heads off for a roll of toilet paper. Randy is grateful when Tony returns. In between blows, he tries to catch his breath.

We all know the real stories inside Randy's sorrow. His father's alcoholic beatings. His mother's overdose. We know not to ask him any questions or have him share anything about his past. The rules on the ranch are clear. Don't dwell on who you were before. Be the person you are becoming.

Randy gasps for air. He is just a sliver of himself, half melted away and shaking. We stay clumped in a tight circle, the mounting box in the middle. Moo holds steady; he hasn't moved an inch. His head is low, about two feet from Randy's face, bending over our bulge of bodies. His eyes are half-closed, ears out to the side of his head, listening. Waiting for Randy to make the next move.

I can't quite look at Randy's face or anyone else's. It's as if my skin has peeled back and left the whole nerve of my body exposed. I fall away. I see myself sitting on the dirt inside our circle and hovering above it at the same time, peering downward at our small world filled with trouble.

"Hey, Randy," Eliza's voice slips in from the silence. "You can take Scout next time; I promise."

WHEN HE'S READY, Randy picks himself up and brushes the dirt off his pants. We push ourselves off the ground alongside him. He shakes like thunder. Someone brings him a glass of water. Randy clears his throat, blows his nose.

"Thanks, guys. Thanks a lot. I'm sorry to freak you guys out. I was just, damn, I don't know. I guess I was scared. You know. He's a big dude. I mean he's cool. I love this dude." He points toward Moo.

"No, Randy. It's cool. We get it. These horses fuckin' freak us all out. Damn, dude, you're good. We got your back," Tony's quick to chime in. He's still uncomfortable with the whole tender show.

Flor walks over to Randy. She looks like a tiny doll standing next to him. She puts her arms around his waist, as much as she can, and pulls him in close. Her head rests just above his rolling belly. The rest of us gather around them. With Flor and Randy in the center, we spread out our arms and create a giant group hug. Touching like this, between men and women, is not allowed on this ranch. We hold on for longer than any of us feel comfortable.

Randy shuffles around the round pen on a short circle, getting his equilibrium back. Moo stands motionless next to the box, reins over the horn, patient and waiting. Randy moves back toward the box, pushes it around in the sand for stability and stands back on top.

I wonder if I should stop him, tell him he has already achieved so much today. But then I look over at Moo. He's standing tall and ready. He is holding to his mission. Moo shuffles his hooves, putting all four feet squarely underneath his big brown body, preparing to balance Randy on top. Randy grabs the reins and Moo's mane. His left boot moves smoothly into the stirrup. He shoves off the box, trying to swing his right leg up and over Moo's rump. He misses. Randy kicks Moo's left hip hard, his size and flexibility still presenting a challenge. Moo stands dead quiet, like a soldier's mount, refusing to let any disturbance rock his concentration. Finally, Randy prods his right leg across Moo's rear end, clears, and lands hard in the saddle. He reaches down to his right and places his off-side boot into the stirrup.

"That's the way to do it," Tony calls to Randy.

Randy looks down at us. His face square and concentrated. Only his eyes show the consequence of surprise. His body swallows his fear. Little driblets of tears still mark his cheeks. No one speaks. Eliza and Flor drag the box out of the round pen. I stand in the middle, watching his hands.

"Pick up the reins, Randy. Moo is waiting for you."

SHE'S NOT READY

Colt Starting / March / 1998

"She's not ready," I scream at the famous trainer and the six other men in cowboy hats who gather around the perimeter of the round pen.

"What?" the famous trainer shouts back to me. The sound of my voice is carried away with the wind. I give him hand motions, body signals, trying to let him know, again, that she's not ready. He's been pushing me to mount her anyhow.

I'm the last to finish my rides and the only woman in this bunch of trainers who has come to this western ranch to study with the famous trainer for these past three weeks. The wind blows fifty miles per hour, but the sun is out. It's a good day. Not the blizzard conditions we've had almost every day since we arrived.

A breeder came through on our first day and dropped a load of young horses in the big corral: an oval-shaped pen not seventy

feet long. Thirty or more colts swirled in the solid-walled tank as
the dirt rose like smoke and dusted their hides. The white edges
of their eyes grew wide around their pupils as we leaned over the
pine planks peering in at them. Our goal was to start four colts
each. The famous trainer went through the herd and picked the
best ones to work with. This one's my last. She's a little filly, all
Arabian, only two years old. No name yet. I've nicknamed her
Terry, after one of my feisty clients back home. The rest of the
men are finished with their rides. All their colts accept the saddle
and have at least ten rides apiece on them. Today they are free to
hang out and watch. The drinking has already begun.

They're clean-cut cowboys. Not a whisker out of place. A few
have the standard rolled mustache I've seen in commercials. Their
words bounce off each other like balls rolling downhill. We've
had only a few short conversations in three weeks.

"How's she coming?" the famous trainer asked me at breakfast
this morning.

"She's real young. And she's not *come through*," I tell him. That's
the language we use. It's trade talk for she doesn't trust me yet.
Working with the famous trainer means I must adapt my language to the group code. "Soft" means she's receptive to pressure
all over her body. "Generous" means she's a quick and easy study.
"Not very generous" means the famous trainer doesn't like the
horse, and therefore no one in the group does. This little filly has
already been sorted into the "not generous" group. For me, I don't
think she's ready. She's not mature enough to handle the pressure
of humans. She has "try," as they like to say. She listens to me and
has worked all the skills I've asked of her. She's learning. But every
day she needs me to start over again. Refresh her mind. Rebuild
her confidence. She's coming, but she's not there yet.

"You're just going to have to ride her through it. Some are

just like that," the famous trainer tells me as he eats his breakfast. He's well-known throughout the country, and the world, as a trainer who takes his time starting young horses. "We don't have the luxury to take more time," he says, biting down on a piece of wheat toast. "We're horse trainers, not counselors. Some you just have to ride out the trouble. If she doesn't come through, you'll have to ride her anyhow." He chews one more piece of bacon while I try to warm myself with a bowl of grits and eggs covered in chili. I nod in agreement because going against the famous trainer is not a good idea. He's got a healthy-sized ego and a pot full of hot anger under its surface. He is a great trainer. Some think he is the best. I've studied with enough of them that I know to keep my mouth shut and nod "yes, sir."

Terry follows me around the pen like a happy puppy. She's soft. Her body bends around me like playdough. She's a short-backed, agile creature, the color of mud mixed with clay, and she stands only up to my shoulders. It took six days to get the buck out of her; every time I put the saddle on she would blow her girth out, round her back, and race around the round pen humped into a ball. Each day got worse until she finally exhausted herself. She carried that saddle around for twelve hours the last day, as per the famous trainer's suggestion. I put it on her around 8:00 a.m. and left it on until dinnertime. In between the other three colts I was starting, I'd check in on her and make sure the cinch was tight. At lunch, I ran her around the arena, riding my older gelding and wagging a bright orange flag at her flanks. The famous trainer said this would get her "quiet." She had foam pushing out from under the saddle blanket by the time I was through with her, but the look in her eyes didn't change—still terrified of that thing strapped to her back. But this approach seemed to have worked, because the following day she stood still when I saddled her. No buck. Not a flinch. Her eyes were empty. No terror. No nothing. Exhausted, I thought. Traumatized, perhaps. Is this what they mean by finally "coming through"? She carried that saddle around like a prisoner hauling trash on the highway.

Back in the pen, I walk over to the famous trainer and drop my eyes to the ground as he tells me what I am going to have to do. Bend her neck, put my foot in the stirrup, bounce up and down off the ground to see how she'll do with my weight. I've been doing this same routine for the last ten days. She goes crazy once she sees me above her. Every time I've left the ground and risen up, with one foot in the stirrup, she yanks her head straight into the air, her back drops down below her withers, her hind legs thrust under her belly. She sees me as a lion on her back. Every time I stand in the stirrup, she gets ready to hump up, bolt off, or both. She's not "making the change." She's not able to decipher that the me who is on the ground is the same me who is climbing on her back. If I swing up and over the saddle, she'll explode. I know this but keep nodding my head at the famous trainer as he tells me to do it again.

I walk back to Terry. She's standing quietly with the wind blowing her tail at such an angle it looks like a long, straight broom. I move onto her left side and bend her neck around with the lead rope and halter. I barely touch her. Her neck curves around me like Gumby. She brushes her wet nostrils onto my coat, holding herself in this position without effort, chewing on the corner pocket of my jeans. Then I reach for the stirrup. Her head and neck snap straight and brace for my next move. I bend her neck around again. This time I put pressure on the lead line and hold her folded in half. I pick up the stirrup, twist it around, and as my foot slides through, she starts to twirl in tight circles around me. I spin and hop, spin and hop, until finally she comes to a stop. I release her head straight again as a reward, scratch her neck, her poll, the side of her face. She stands wide and hard, ready to flee. I repeat myself and start the process over. Maybe ten more times, until she stops her twirling and allows me to stand up in the stirrup, hovering over her back. I have her neck bent so tight to the side of her body she could fall over if she takes one step. I'd like to release her, let her stand free with me standing above her, but I know she'll take off if I let go. Instead I just bop up and down in the stirrup, as the famous trainer suggested, while I take away all her power by breaking her body in half.

The voice in my head is loud: *She's still not ready. Not coming through. Not generous. Not making the change.* The other trainers leave the rail and head toward their trucks. The back pockets of their Wranglers reveal round packages of tobacco chew. Each man wears a fancy silk cowboy neck scarf, tied neatly into a decorative bow, beneath their Carhart jackets. They are onto their third beer and it's not even lunchtime.

"You're only as good as your toolbox," an older trainer once said to me. I was thirty-one, and my toolbox felt small. I came here to get a bigger box but now felt crammed into something smaller than my own.

The famous trainer keeps nodding his head, motioning me to swing up. I do. In one fluid stroke, I'm on top. Terry twirls round and round. I don't even think to let her straighten out of my bent grip. She's spinning faster and faster. Tighter and tighter. My left hand holds her head to my knee, my right hand reaches back and grabs the back of the saddle. The men run back from their trucks, beers in hand. Hooting and whooping like cowboys at the rodeo.

Terry is spinning herself into a hole. I'm trying to get my right foot into the outside stirrup. She trips and goes down on one knee, knocks my whole body forward and I lose my grip on the lead rope. She's off. Straight-necked and barreling around the round pen. *Ride out the trouble. Ride out the trouble*, I keep repeating to myself as she gets faster and faster, peeling circles around the seventy-foot pen. The men, the famous trainer, they're all a blur. I can't see them, can't hear them. It's just me and Terry. Terry, who is absolutely traumatized by this thing on her back that is me.

She's running to the left, and my right foot, still out of the stirrup, gets hung up on one of the round-pen rails. My knee twists hard as my leg gets dragged backward. Terry bolts even faster from the sound and feel of me getting caught on the rail. She trips again, at a full gallop, and goes down on both knees. I'm whiplashed forward. I lose hold of the cantle. She jumps up. I'm still on top, but now sitting on a giant ball that is bucking and twirling. Bucking and twirling. I spin off. Straight into the round-pen wall. I throw my arms at the wall to protect my head from smashing into the pipe corral rails. Then I'm down flat, in four inches of dirt. Terry's across the pen facing me at a standstill.

The other trainers rush over the top rail and help sit me up. My right knee is quickly filling with fluid and there's a deep gash across my left palm. The blood is studded with bits of manure and dirt. I sit up, spit the sand out of my mouth, and say, "Well, it could have been worse." But then I see Terry walk off. And realize it is worse. She's lame. Not able to bear much weight on her right front leg. I stand and hobble over to her, pulling the lead line out of the sand. Puke wads my esophagus and I swallow hard to keep it down. I walk Terry out to the center of the pen and check her over. There's no swelling, yet. It's probably a tendon sprain, maybe a tear. If it were a break, she wouldn't be able to bear weight on it at all. I'm pissed. Mad at myself. Mad at the wind. Mad at every man in a cowboy hat.

"It'd be good if you could at least sit back on her, you know, for a moment." The famous trainer is in the pen standing right next to me.

"Just for a moment," I say.

I know why this is important. I know leaving her with this last memory of terror isn't how I want her to remember me. I bend Terry around. The famous trainer leaves the pen. I put my left foot in the stirrup and hop up and down off my right leg, which is throbbing and swollen. Terry doesn't take a step. I bend her tight, swing my leg over the saddle, sit down hard, then swing back off in one solid movement. "That's it. That's all for today," I tell the trainer. I take Terry's lead line and labor toward the gate.

November / 2013

Eliza swings up on Billy and tries to take her around the course. We've set up tires, barrels, logs, cones, and small jumps all over the twelve-acre pasture. Billy's busy watching all the other horses run through the course, not thinking for one second about the person on her back. Billy's never been able to pay attention to any one thing too long, and today she's in good company. Because of trauma and the aftereffects of drug addiction, Eliza and many of the other residents on this ranch struggle with attention deficit disorder.

Billy trots twenty feet then stops, swings her head and neck off to the right to look at Tony and Hawk go through the tires. Hawk drops his head low to the ground as he puts one hoof at a time inside the tire wells. He looks like a bulky defensive lineman doing an agility test. Eliza kicks at Billy's side and takes the extra length of her reins to slap Billy on the rump. Billy hops her lithe brown body into the air then takes off again at a trot. They head toward the barrels with the colored flags blowing out from their center. Billy takes one look at the flags, stops, spins, and heads back toward the barn. Eliza bends Billy's neck around and points her again at the flags. Billy's ears pin straight at the blustery menace. She halts again, crow hops, then rears up on her hind legs. When she comes down, Eliza bends her around and turns her in tight circles.

"Take her to the cones first," I yell to Eliza.

Eliza turns to listen to me, then trots over. "She's got a mind like a sieve. Everything just falls out. She knows better, too. Damn, she's stubborn."

Eliza has found her voice and her body. Working the horses has changed her. She no longer pulls out her eyebrows, no longer twirls her hair into knots. Her skin, her eyes, her mouth— everything has a different texture. It looks like she's had cosmetic surgery. She has come back to life. The horses woke her up. Besides Luna, Billy is our most challenging horse. I decided a few months ago to give Billy to the ranch. She is athletic. She can be contrary. She gives away nothing for free.

"She's getting to you," I tell Eliza. "You can't be the leader if you're thinking like her." I laugh a little, then send them toward the cones. If they ride a few series of figure eights, circles, and spirals around the cones, they'll both have calmed down enough to face the flags.

Tony and Hawk have finished the course now. We've had it set up for a month, spread out wide in the pasture, to test the residents' skills and give the horses something to focus on. Tony swings off Hawk and gives Randy the reins. Randy just finished riding Moo around the course a few times and has tied him back at my trailer. He recently graduated to riding Hawk. Randy's still on his diet; he's lost another twenty pounds. He is now able to push off his handmade box and swing over Hawk's back, landing lightly in the saddle. Hawk, he tells me, is his new favorite horse.

Rex and Paul are working with Estrella, touching her all over her body with a blue tarp. Estrella spooks hard when she hears the sound of plastic. Last week Rex opened a candy wrapper while he was on top of her and she took off at a gallop, straight back to her pen. The saddle slid off to the side of her rib cage, but Rex hung on. Today Rex and Paul have decided to desensitize her to things that blow and rattle. They're helping her build confidence. She looks curious. Her ears take their turn flicking on and off the crinkled, flapping fabric. Building confidence in a young horse is a slow process. They are teaching her how to trust them, even when she becomes frightened. They have the saddle thrown over the top rail of the round pen behind them. Once she's quiet and accepts the tarp, they'll saddle her and ride her all over the ranch.

Behind them, I see Sarah and Scout in the round pen. Scout's saddled and bridled, and it looks like Sarah's thinking about mounting. I walk over toward the pen. Sarah doesn't look up. This is her first day back to the horses in almost three months, and she's not speaking with anyone. I've been trying to give her space, but what I really want is to give her a hug and let her know how much I've missed her.

She was close to being kicked off the ranch for screwing one of the male residents in the hay barn. Someone caught them and turned them in. She spent four days on the bench and another six weeks on a solitary contract. Here, at the ranch, a solitary contract is not confinement. It is sixteen-hour workdays cleaning the bathrooms, scrubbing the floors, and washing the dishes after breakfast, lunch, and dinner. Those residents put on long contracts like Sarah's always have a peer with them every minute of the day. They cannot speak with anyone except this peer, and then only to ask questions. Long contracts are meant to have a strict effect. Everyone knows getting kicked off the ranch means breaking parole. And breaking parole means they are heading back to prison.

Sarah reaches down and checks each one of Scout's hooves for rocks. I see her moving her lips and whispering to him. His ears twist around and face backward. He's trying to catch the sounds coming from Sarah's mouth. She's humming or singing some tune. It's faint and high. She sounds like a little girl singing to her stuffed animals, alone in her room. Scout rolls his tongue and yawns.

"Sarah, how are you doing? Are you getting ready to ride?" I ask her. Yes, she nods, but doesn't look at me. "You'll stay in the round pen and work on your turns, your halt, a little bit of canter. Okay?" Yes, another nod. Before Sarah went on contract, Scout was her favorite horse to ride. She is a natural rider, with a good seat. Scout was the first horse she had ridden since she left her family's ranch when she was fourteen years old. She rides Scout like she's been riding horses her whole adult life.

I walk back into the pasture and head over toward the jumps. Eliza has Billy at a nice lope, jumping the two cross bars without any trouble.

"You want me to raise them?" I ask her.

"Where's she going?" Eliza looks past me and on up the road.

Sarah's out of the round pen and galloping up the road toward the main office. Her reins are long and dangle down Scout's neck. She races past Rex and Paul who just mounted Izzy and Estrella. Estrella spooks from behind as Sarah flies by. Paul stays quiet in the saddle as he pulls Estrella into tight circles, trying to keep her calm.

"What the hell are you doing? Bend him around. Sarah. Fuck, Sarah, bend him around," Rex screams at her as she races by.

"Aw shit, Sarah," I say under my breath, and take off running across the pasture over to where Moo is standing tied at my trailer. I grab my lariat from inside the tack-room door and throw it over the horn as I swing up. I see Sarah and Scout pass the cottonwoods on the far west side of the pasture. I take off at an angle through the field on Moo, trying to judge how the hell I can cut her off. From a nearby neighbor's pasture, I hear sandhill cranes calling, their muffled songs sounding like French horns sending out a warning.

I see Tony from the corner of my eye, running up the road, straight at Sarah, screaming at the top of his lungs. "Bend him. Bend him. What the hell are you doing, Sarah? Bend him around."

Sarah barely touches the reins. She's heading toward the shop area. Stacks of lumber are piled up in the middle of the road and she's not even attempting to steer away from them. Even from far away I can see her cheeks are rose-colored and flushed. They look like tiny, round, flashing red lights glowing in the distance. The rest of her face looks pale and pasty. I lean farther up Moo's neck, and we race toward the wood pile. If I can get there before Sarah, I can use the pile of rough-cut pine boards from the local sawmill as a wall to slow them down. Scout has his neck stretched out flat and smooth, pulling taut from his withers. He's loping at a good clip, not as fast as he can go, but a steady three-beat thumping knocks loud against packed earth. When I get close to him, I can tell by his half-closed eyes that he's not in a panic. I send Moo right for the stacked lumber jutting out onto the road. We arrive at such an angle that the wall of wood and Moo's body create a tight corner. Scout heads right at us. His head and neck rise from his withers. His eyes tighten into slits. His hindquarters coil and lift his forehand as he rolls into our corner, like a boat coming into harbor. Sarah falls forward onto his neck from the unexpected deceleration. Scout comes to a halt, nickers, then walks forward a few steps and lays his head across Moo's neck. Sarah looks up with a snarl.

"They hate me. They all hate me. Everything I do, they're out to get me." As she talks, I open the loop of my lariat and slip it over Scout's head. "I don't trust any of them. This horse is the only one I trust."

She looks terrible. Her hair is all stringy, greasy. Her teeth look tan next to her skin and one is missing. There's a gap between her upper right incisor and her first molar that I've never noticed before.

I neck rein Moo around and walk back up the road. My rawhide tether is loose around Scout's neck as he follows by my side. Sarah drops the reins and slumps forward like a monkey on his back. Her arms dangle from her sides, with a fist at each end.

"I've been worried about you, Sarah," I tell her as we walk side by side, swaying in rhythm like clothes on a line. She looks up ahead of us. Her eyes are fixed in place with eyebrows pinching around them. I see her chest rise and fall in quick succession. She looks like she's going to scream. We pass the cottonwoods and turn the corner of the ranch loop. Scout curves his body into the turn, and Sarah's head falls off center. Her body goes limp, rocking like a drunken sailor on the wave of Scout's lumbering spine. She looks like she could roll right off.

"Why did you do it, Sarah?" She shifts her eyes to me but never turns her head. She knows I'm asking about what happened in the hay barn.

"Taking my clothes off for men is all I've ever done," she mumbles, never looking up.

Sarah started working at her relative's strip club at the age of thirteen. She learned to dye her hair, plaster on makeup, and dance the pole, her skinny girlish legs wrapping around its circumference.

Everyone meets us back at the barn.

"What do you think you're doing, Sarah? You know the rules." Still on top of Izzy, with Paul riding next to him, Rex is at her height and screaming into her face. She stares ahead without a blink. When we first started riding the horses, Scout, Hawk, and Willie all had the bad habit of bolting off, with their rider hanging on for dear life. If a horse takes off with you, the rule is, you must bend their neck around until they stop. Rex turns Izzy away from her, cussing under his breath.

"Sarah, what's wrong?" Paul asks. "You can ride Scout better than that." Randy takes a good look at her, then looks away. Tony does the same thing. They turn and walk away from us, scuffing the ground with their boots, heads tilted to the ground. I turn Moo to the right and head across the pasture toward the jumps, with Sarah and Scout still walking by our side. Eliza and Billy come toward us.

"You want to go for a ride together, Sarah?" Eliza asks.

"Not just yet," I tell Eliza. "Give us some time."

Colt Starting / 1998

"Jorge's on his way over to get her, Ginger," the famous trainer tells me as Terry and I limp out the gate.

"I've got her. I'll take her to the barn," I tell him.

I open the gate, and Terry follows me out. We walk across the wind-whipped clay, slipping on the frozen spots, trying to hold our balance. We hitch ourselves along like an old married couple.

Both of us too young to be hurting this badly. I'm thinking about ice, where I can get some and how to wrap my knee and Terry's tendon. I've got a long pair of socks back at my trailer that will work. I'll cut the toes out and pull it up her leg. Fold it half-down and make a tube that I can fill with ice. Fifteen minutes of ice, on and off, for the next few hours. In my first-aid kit, I have pain-killers for both of us and enough vet wrap and bandages to wrap both our legs for the night.

When I walk into the barn, Jorge gives me a gentle smile and reaches for the lead rope. I hand Terry over to him. "I'll be right back," I say and head out to get what I need. At my trailer, I down three ibuprofen and wrap an ace bandage over my jeans and around my knee. I grab the sock and first-aid kit, then head to the bunkhouse to get some ice. I'm walking back to the barn when I meet up with a few of the other trainers.

"You want us to make you a sandwich or something?" they ask. It's lunchtime on the final day of our time here. Everyone will be loading up horse trailers and tack this afternoon in preparation for leaving early tomorrow morning.

"No, thanks. I'm not hungry," I tell them. Their hats are pulled low over their foreheads and I can't see their eyes. They walk on with hunched-over shoulders, shuffling their Red Wings or Ariats with their toes pointing out to the side.

Terry's tied just inside the barn, and Jorge is shoveling wood shavings into a stall, making a soft bed so Terry can rest for the night. I walk through the double barn door. She turns her head at me and nickers. She's placing some weight on her right front leg. I get the anti-inflammatory paste out of my kit and squeeze a few grams between her lips and onto her tongue. She licks, chews, and swallows a few times.

She stands with one hind leg cocked, then shifts her weight

onto all four and lets me pick up her hoof and pull the sock up her leg. I fold the sock down from the knee to make the tube and fill it with ice. Then I secure the vet wrap around the length of her tendon to hold the ice pack in place. I sit back on one of the hay bales nearby and put the leftover bag of ice on my knee. My left hand is throbbing and needs a good cleaning, but it's not too bad. Just a cut. No stitches, I think to myself.

"You alright?" I can see the silhouette of the famous trainer in the doorway, with the sun bright behind his back. All the women I know love him, but I didn't come here to fall in love. Other trainers, men I know from home, suggested that I spend some time around him.

I wonder now what he thinks about my ride, my fall. I don't ask, and a big part of me doesn't care. I know he would have been able to stay on top of Terry. He can ride anything and make the most difficult ride look easy. I must have looked like a tattered rag flying off her back.

"Yeah, I'm alright," I say.

"What'd you learn today?" he asks.

"That I'd better start listening better. That little mare, she's got a lot to teach me."

He looks down at his watch and calls for Jorge in Spanish to come help unload hay from his truck, then turns away, never meeting my eye.

November / 2013

"You want a bite?" I ask Sarah and pull a strip of elk jerky from a small saddlebag I've got strapped to the cantle. Sarah twists and looks at the back of my saddle. She points behind the bag to a long, braided ponytail tied to the saddle skirt.

"What's that?" she asks.

I'm surprised she noticed. She hasn't asked me a question or shown any sign of interest in anything or anyone all afternoon.

"That," I turn and lift the bundle of hair and caress it in my hand, "well, that is Domecq," I say.

"Who's Domecq?"

I let the bundle fall back to the saddle. Moo's fluid, undulating walk has the blond braid swishing back and forth alongside his golden-brown flank.

"He was a stallion I cared for over the last ten years. I had to put him down a few months ago. That's his mane. Part of it."

Domecq was over thirty years old when I put him down. I was his primary caregiver. I watched him wither away this past summer to skin and bones. There wasn't anything more I could do for him, except make the hard decision to let him go. I walked him past the mares one last time, on his way up the pasture, to the place I chose to lay him down. He puffed himself into a stud as we passed the girls. *Arruff, ruff, ruff.* Grunting and calling. The mares squealing, *eeallll*, and swirling around in their pens as we passed.

Domecq was a champion distance racing horse. He spent most of his competitive years running across the Sierra Nevadas, the Rocky Mountains of Colorado, across the peaks of the Sangre de Cristo Mountains in northern New Mexico. I came to care for him in his later years as a standing stallion for one of the horse farms where I work.

Sarah can't stop staring at Domecq's flaxen braid. Her eyes open with curiosity, and for the first time today she shows me that grin I've come to lean on.

"You kept part of him?"

"Yeah, I guess I did. I mean, I wasn't sure how to get on with-out him. I just carry him around now. It makes me feel like he's still with me. Makes me feel stronger. Sometimes I have some hard, fucked-up days, Sarah. I need help sometimes. We all do."

She pivots around in the saddle and faces forward. We see Eliza and Billy back by the barn, awaiting our arrival.

"Can you bring me a photo of him, please? I want to see him. He must have been—" Her voice trails off as she turns again to look at me.

"He was the best part of my workday for the last ten years," I tell her, as I wipe my eyes with the back of my sleeve.

"I'm sorry, Ginger. It'll be alright," she assures me. She sits straight up in the saddle and picks up Scout's reins for the first time today.

Colt Starting / 1998

My Ford diesel idles as I load my gelding into the trailer. The air is dry and crisp. For the first time in three weeks, the wind is not blowing. The sky is turquoise. Not a puff of cloud in sight. Spring may be starting to finally poke its head through this soil, but I'm heading home. Three days driving south through some of the most beautiful parts of the west, hauling myself and my gelding back to New Mexico.

I shut my cab door and turn the heat to high. It's twelve degrees above zero at eight o'clock in the morning. I drive past the barn, the corrals and round pens. Just ahead of me I see the breeder's rig, pulled off to the right, where the famous trainer has been loading all the "broke" horses into the clamoring metal container. There must be twenty or more horses stuffed into the skin of that rig.

Out the back, I see him working her. Back and forth on a tight circle. She's the last to load. Still with the vet wrap support around her right leg. The overnight rest, the medicine, ice—all of it has helped. She's not quite as lame. But she doesn't want to load, either. She's the last to be squeezed into a space so tight, it brings out the fight in her all over again.

I drive up slowly and come to a stop behind them, about fifty feet away. I turn down the heater and watch him work her. She's sweating. Steam rises off her back. Her owner, the woman who dropped all of them off three weeks ago, is off to the side, far away, hoping to keep herself from being trampled. Her skin is weathered. She holds her back straight. Her arms fold tightly across her chest. *Proud with a mix of privilege*, I think to myself. Proud yet dependent on him, the famous trainer, to get this mare, the not so generous one, finally loaded into her trailer.

I roll down the passenger side window and look over toward where the owner is standing. She's not looking at me. Her eyes are focused on the famous trainer. His instruction is all she wants. I want to tell her that her filly isn't ready to be ridden. That she tried to show me, but I rode her anyhow. I didn't listen.

I roll up the window, put the truck into low gear, and drive past Terry, who is still refusing to put one hoof into that rig. I wish I was more like her. That clear. That certain. I wish I could trust my instincts like she does. I wish I had fought harder for what I knew. *Ginger*, I tell myself, *next time you will.*

November / 2013

"Did she tell you?" Tony asks me.

"Tell me what?" I say.

Tony and Randy have known Sarah since the day she entered this ranch. Those who come onto the ranch around the same time period are referred to as peers. When they hit their eighteenth month of living on the ranch, they are required to tell every detail of their entire life. It's called Dissipation. Peers sit in a room full of mentors and elders for three straight days. From early morning and long into the night, each peer has their turn. They take as long as needed to tell every painful, embarrassing detail of every terrible thing they have ever done. Tony, Randy, and Sarah know each other very well.

"I don't know if I should say this or not," Tony continues.

"She should know," Randy says.

"Know what? Come on. It's been hard enough today," I answer, leaning back against the round-pen rail as I watch Eliza and Sarah walk away from us, stepping up the road on Billy and Scout.

"When Sarah was in prison," Tony says, "she was beaten pretty bad. You know, by the women in her pod. Left to die."

"That's why she's so messed up. That's why her leg looks like that. The guards found her," Randy tells me. "I think these last few months have sent her back into that hole. That's what it seems like to me, anyhow. Man, it's hard to go back, Ms. Ginger. Go back to some of the places we all have been."

I leave Randy and Tony and hustle over to Moo to remount.

"I'll be right back," I tell them, then lope up the road toward

Sarah and Eliza. They turn their horses around to face me when they hear our hoofbeats coming. "Wait a minute," I say as I swing off Moo. I move around to Moo's hindquarters and untie Domecq's braided mane from the skirt of my saddle. Moo stands quiet with the reins slack around his neck. I slide around Scout's hindquarters and pick up one of the saddle ties behind the cantle. I wrap the thin leather around Domecq's hair and tie it into a knot around the root end of the braid. Sarah watches from up above.

A little color has come back to her face. She reaches around and holds Domecq in her hand. His shiny golden mane dangles from her palm.

"Thank you, Ginger. Thank you for everything." Her face is solemn and lost in thought.

"You know, Ginger, I'm half-broke. I need these walls. These fences." Her arms wave wide, marking a full circumference of this ranch.

I KNOW SHE'S RIGHT. She's not ready to be on her own. And I don't know if she will ever be.

CROOKED LINE

February / 2014

The smell of alfalfa blends with diesel smoke and chokes the cold morning air. I'm watching Richard Sanchez in the front seat of his king-cab Ford truck fussing with a torn sheet of paper and his calculator. Two hundred bales times eight dollars, plus delivery fee. He's covered in a light-green dust; it sticks to the sides of his nostrils under his drooping eyeglasses. His hair is a curly black nest stuffed under his sweat-stained baseball cap.

"Eeeeh. I don't know. I may have to go up on my bales. This diesel is killing me." He looks at me from under his thick brown glasses. "Plus the tractor repairs, the truck and trailer tires, eeeeh, there's no money in it." He complains in his usual way.

Tony and Randy are busy cleaning out the hay barn. They have pulled out all the remaining bales from last September's final cut, trying to make room for the new hay Richard has delivered.

Randy pushes the broom over the wooden-planked floor made of thin and graying pine boards. A black, moldy cloud of old alfalfa debris puffs out the door.

"$1,750," Richard announces. "I'll only charge you half my delivery fee." I smile and thank him. His farm is two miles north of this ranch. He charges us the same delivery price that he charges when he hauls to Santa Fe, one hour away. Not complaining about price is an essential part of keeping the hay grower happy.

"Thank you, Richard." I take off my gloves and shake his hand. "Tony, can you run down to headquarters with this bill and pick up a check for Richard?"

Tony gives me a nod, swipes at the front of his jeans, and stomps the tiny green flakes off his boots.

"Can you give me a lift up to the office?" Tony asks Richard.

"Jump in," Richard says and shoves to the floorboard of his truck his grease-stained Carhart jacket, a pile of old newspapers, and a broken cardboard box filled with washers, nails, and empty Styrofoam coffee cups. Tony climbs in, and the truck blows a cough of diesel through its knocking muffler.

"Nice and green." Randy goes over to the fresh hay and takes a giant whiff. He bends from the waist and pulls a grab of alfalfa from a bale. "Old Richard has some nice hay, no?"

"Let's get this loaded into the barn. Is it all cleaned up?" I ask.

"Yep. And I raked up some of the scraps for the ducks, too." He points to a pile of loose hay mounded in front of the cottonwood. "These bales are heavy. Can we ask Rex or Paul to help us out?"

I shrug my shoulders and shake my head sideways. Two hundred bales are not too many for two people to stack. Randy's always looking for ways to make life easier.

"You bring them in; I'll stack," I tell him. Randy walks over to put his gloves back on, then picks up the first fresh bale. He comes through the door, takes a few heavy steps across the pine boards, and one of the boards pops free and smacks him hard on top of his kneecap.

"Ahhh! You goddamn motherfucker." He falls to his knees and lands belly first on the hay bale. "What a bitch." He grabs at his knee, turns, then sits on the bale.

There goes my worker, I think to myself. Randy doesn't recover quickly from things that surprise or hurt him. Underneath his beefy frame, he's fragile. I'll have to wait, let him rub his pain away and listen to him moan. Tony comes through the door almost at a run. He's the opposite of Randy, always ready to work hard, to take on a new challenge. He's already dragging a new bale into the barn, when he stops in front of the hole in the floor.

"What the hell happened here?" He bends over and picks up the board.

"Fuckin' thing swung up and bit me," Randy announces.

Tony goes into the tack room and gets a hammer. He bangs out the old nails and kneels to put the board back in place.

"Huh. What the fuck?" Tony takes the hammer, twists the end around and rips out another board, next to the missing plank. Then the next board after that.

"What are you doing?" I ask Tony.

"I think there's something down there. Can you get me your cell phone? I need the flashlight."

Randy crawls off his bale and leans over the gap in the floorboards. He pushes his head down close to the hole. "It's a box."

I turn my cell phone's flashlight feature on and shine it into the dark space. There's a black box sitting in the dust under the floorboards, a foot below.

"These boards are pulling up way too easy," Tony says. "Someone's put this box here pretty recent." He keeps pulling more boards until there is space enough to release the box. Randy reaches down and lifts the box, then sits it down on the fresh bale. It is covered in a light dust, and the lid is latched with a twisted paperclip. I swipe the top of the box clean.

The hay barn is locked daily, along with the equipment shed. Only livestock members have access to the key that is kept at the front desk, under supervision, with all the other important keys for the ranch. Tony and Randy look at me. I am the obvious choice for who should open the box. They step back three feet, trying to keep their distance, but still bending toward the box with anticipation. Their faces stretch with worry. Tony taps his fingers impatiently against his thighs.

I lift the lid. Inside sit three 6cc syringes filled with a cloudy liquid. The needle applicators are locked in place. An open bag of condoms lies next to the syringes. A half-full metal jar of a gray-white powder sits on top of a few packs of cigarettes. Three rolled joints spin around on the bottom. As I rummage through the box, my hands start to shake.

"We're fucked," Tony states with certainty.

"No fucking kidding," Randy snaps.

I shut the lid, twist the paperclip into lock position, and set it down on the bale. I grab my upper lip with my right hand and pinch it tightly.

"What should we do?" asks Randy. Tony is now pounding his fist on his thighs.

I don't answer. Staring at the box, I feel my temples start to pulse. "Let's get these bales in and stacked," I tell the guys, standing up quickly. Then I pick up the box and walk out to my truck, placing the box on the front passenger seat.

"I can't fucking believe this shit." Tony knows finding this box will change everything. This box commands great power on this ranch. It is an undercover sex and drug cache, something that can be found in almost every prison. Randy and Tony have spent many years in prison. They understand, they recognize, far more than I, what this box represents.

They start pulling in the bales. We heave and stack them from the back corner of the shed toward the door, leaving exposed the gaping hole in the floorboard. We move faster than usual, sweat dripping off our chins and noses. The bales weigh at least sixty pounds each. We are silent as we work. I'm thinking hard about what to do next. When we finish, the guys sit briefly on the last two bales. Their heaving chests pump up and down, and I can see veins popping from their necks above their shirt lines. I stand facing them. Green dust sticks to the sweat dripping down my arms.

"I'll go find James and Daniel." I wipe the crust of alfalfa off my face. "You guys better get back to work. I wouldn't talk about this to anyone right now. Keep it quiet." But I know they will spread the news; secrets don't last a minute on this ranch.

I drive over to the ranch office looking for Daniel. I am told he's busy in the Vatican room, the room where residents go when they have broken ranch rules, waiting on their contracts or punishment for misbehaviors. I get back in my truck and head across the property. The residents wave to me from their work stations, curious about my irregular activity away from the horses. I park near the dining hall and tuck the box under my sweat-stained denim shirt. The dining hall is empty, and the sound of my footsteps echoes off the thick adobe walls. Past the check-in desk, I turn and walk the long, thin hallway that leads to three different doorways. A chair sits outside the second doorway, and I hear the muffled voices of James and Daniel inside. I sit down and slide the box under my chair, out of sight.

Inside, James and Daniel are talking slowly. They ask questions to another man, whose voice I can't identify. There are long pauses and what seems like indecision or hesitation, then soft, quiet answers are fed back to James and Daniel by a voice so little it sounds like a child's. *Could he be the one?* I think to myself. Then I shove the box farther back under my seat. I hear three chairs squeak backward, indicating a conclusion to the meeting. The shuffle of feet follows and the doorknob turns. A young man with short, cropped red hair and bushy eyebrows leaves the room first and turns toward me. He bows his head as he passes but doesn't say hello. Daniel and James walk out behind him and stop in surprise to see me sitting there. I stand up and face them, waiting a few seconds for the redhead to move farther down the hall.

"I need to speak with you guys." I bend over and slide the box out from under the chair. "I have to show you something."

"Come on in." Daniel waves me forward and walks back through the open door. James turns behind me, and we duck down to enter.

The room has no windows. It is shaped like an oval, with chairs circling the perimeter, reminiscent of an AA or NA meeting. Each chair is placed at just the right angle where everyone can meet the eye of every participant. I sit on the first empty chair next to James. He scuffs his chair back a few inches and turns it slightly toward me. I lay the box on my lap, placing both palms flat against the top. I tap my nails nervously against its surface. It could be a jewelry box. A box of candles. It could be filled with intricate glass beads. Someone's prized possession.

"What do you have there, Ginger?" James asks me.

Daniel leans forward, elbows resting on his knees. Both of their faces are empty of stress. Whatever happened in this room with this young redheaded man who just exited has given them relief. I wish I could do the same.

"I'm sorry, guys. I found this. In the hay barn. Just now. Under the floorboards. Under, you know, where we store the hay."

My fingers pluck at the paperclip holding the box shut. It sounds like a tiny cymbal.

"Tony and Randy were helping me load the new hay into the barn when we found it." I twist the paperclip and open the lid. I lift off my chair and walk over toward James and lay the box down on his lap. He squeezes his knees shut to create a cradle, then he meets my eye. I start backing away, pinching my lips together and shaking my head.

"I'm sorry. Really sorry, guys. I don't know who, or how, or when this went down."

Daniel and James bend over the box. Their fingers push the contents around, rolling their pointer fingers over the syringes and joints. Daniel stands up and slaps his hand against a small tabletop that holds the only lamp in the room. The light rattles and flickers as if the earth is quaking underneath us. His nostrils flare out to the side. His mouth quivers where his cheeks meet his lips. Under his breath he mutters, "You've got to be fuckin' kidding me."

"What in the hell?" James picks up the box in two hands and drops it, then lifts his hands to his head. The contents lie in a loose pile on the floor. Each ingredient has its own contour, its own space, making the quantity of drugs look larger than I had originally thought.

They look up at me and bark out questions. "When? Where? Who has seen this?"

"It was just Randy and Tony with me stacking hay when we found it under the loose floorboards."

Daniel takes the edge of his collar and wipes his upper lip. James pokes the joints and syringes around the floor with the toe of his boot.

"Yeah . . . well, yeah, Ginger. This is us. This is who we are. You already know, we're some of the most fucked-up people. The worst you'll ever meet." Daniel folds his shoulders and slumps forward from his core. "We'll need to get moving on this quickly. Only Randy and Tony know about it?" He straightens his back and sits up.

With that, James leans forward and places everything back in the box, then shuts the lid. He twists the paperclip until it snaps into pieces and falls to the ground. He tucks the box under his arm and starts toward the door.

"We'll be right back," James says, motioning for Daniel to follow. Outside in the hall, the thick adobe walls make their voices sound like hound dogs baying in the distance. The low notes pause and repeat, emphasizing their confusion, their pain, their need for a decision.

I have always known I don't belong here. I've never once pointed a needle at my veins, nor had the urge to. Never has one of my parents or siblings overdosed in front of me. No one I know has crashed or wrecked a car from alcoholism or drug addiction or spent time in prison for smashing a man's head in because he looked at them too closely. I have never panhandled for change on street corners or broken into cars and homes because I was desperate for a hit. Stealing for any reason is beyond my comprehension. My brain doesn't work like theirs. I don't know anything about their brains, their bodies. They are ruled by different instincts.

The door swings open and James leans his head through the jamb. "Ginger, we need to go to headquarters, find the rest of the council, and tell them what's going on. I think, Daniel and I think, maybe you should go home for the day. We'll take care of this from here, but we do thank you for coming to us. I'm sorry you have been brought into the middle of this."

He's halfway out the door before I can ask him, "It's the live-stock team, isn't it?" He gives me a nod and is gone.

MY DOGS GREET ME as I drive through my gate. Was it my fault? What didn't I notice? Was I not paying attention? Taking things for granted? I have lived in this valley for over twenty years. I've been robbed four times. Saddles, bridles, irrigation pumps, TVs, and computers have all been stolen. I'm not naïve about where I live and who I live around. This river valley, just forty minutes north of Santa Fe, has been dealing with the blight of poverty and drug addiction much longer than the rest of the states. We go back three or four generations of families who have made their living off drugs. Shortly after my last break-in, I bought a gun. In a fit of anger, I went out to the back of my property and shot holes in old beer cans for an hour. I wanted everyone to hear that gun popping off and bullets flying.

My blue heeler nips at the bottom edge of my jeans. She wants to do something, but I tell her to stay, as I enter the horse corral and halter my gray gelding, Izzy. The sun is high in the sky. It's 3:00 in the afternoon, and I don't know what to do with myself. On my way home, I called Glenda and told her everything. She's the only one who knows how much the people at this ranch mean to me. She's always said, the horses are what turned our relation-ship around. She knows how horses, all on their own, can change people's lives.

I pick at the rocks embedded in Izzy's hooves. I need Izzy today. I need his back, his legs, his endless ability to stay present. I decide to go for a ride.

I throw a small saddlebag over the horn and toss in my cell phone and water bottle. I motion to the dogs to lie down and stay. They question me, with their bellies flat against the warm barnyard dirt, ready to spring forward in unison with my slightest gesture. "I'll be back in a few hours," I say. Usually I bring the dogs, but today I want to move out fast. I know they will need water and periods of rest to keep up with Izzy. The pace will be too much for them. I raise both of my hands in a strong, flat signal. It puts a wall between us. The three dogs lie down in the corral dirt and rest their heads on their paws as I leave out the back gate atop Izzy.

It's easy in big open land to forget about myself. The sun beats down on brome grass, the yucca, my forehead, and dried sagebrush indiscriminately. We are all made of the same tissue under the unforgiving canopy of a wide open western sky. The reins slip into the creases between my thumb and first finger, the folded skin matches the cracking bark on juniper trees. Izzy's back is round and stable, like these hills heading east into the mountains. When I get in a tangle, when I can't think through things straight, I almost always get on a horse. Belle taught me, long ago, that riding horses creates order in my body. Every molecule falls back into its rightful place, even as the world seems to break apart around me.

How could this have happened? I knew Sarah had her struggles, but Rex? Omar? Paul? Paul, whose eyes were so bright, clear, and sharp. Who told me the first time I met him that he would be the first in his family to rid himself of the cycle of prison. And Flor? She was the stellar leader of the group. Always

holding counsel when someone was having a bad day. I feel the
tension of the day take up residence in my chest. I push Izzy into
a gallop, and we head up the arroyo hitting twenty miles per
hour. His flaxen mane whips against his neck as the wind pen-
etrates the holes in my dirty, overworked Carhart.

We make two turns, first north then east, and head toward the
ammo grounds where men in camouflage pull the trigger at broken TV sets. Izzy hears the popping and skids sideways with each
shot. My left hamstring cramps and grabs me back on center. He's
hot underneath me. Already I feel the sweat of the saddle stick to
his back. My jeans fit wet and tight around my crotch.

Heading east, away from gunshots, we'll merge with the Rio
de Ancha, the wide, dry arroyo that rolls west from Truchas to
the Rio Grande. We climb the first hill and Izzy digs in with his
hindquarters. It's a scramble of push and pull, as his front and
hind legs work in unison to motor us up the deep sandy incline.
I lift over his neck to get my weight in just the right place where
I won't throw him off balance. I squeeze my quadriceps to his rib
cage harder than usual. I need his body to hold me. My legs tremble with weakness I don't recognize. I grip him like a climber
holds the rock face.

I remember Sarah, on her six-week contract for getting caught
having sex in the hay barn. Now, I wonder, who turned her in?
How long has this been going on? I think about how mad Sarah
was on her return to livestock. How she couldn't trust anyone.
Why didn't she rat them out? Why didn't she break her silence,
come clean, and let Daniel and James know what was really
going on? Maybe now she will. Maybe she will tell everything
and keep her place on the ranch secure.

On top of the ridge, Izzy sniffs and puffs, catching his breath
and searching for life in this barren landscape. We see tracks.

Jackrabbit, deer, cow, calf, and elk. They are loose on this barbed-wire-less landscape. I look down to see who we might meet. Who will notice us? Who will know we are here?

I look up and see a hint of orange and gray. It slides between the cholla and piñon. Coyote up the hill. Two beats at a trot. An unhurried pace. He shifts his body inside the blending sagebrush, his tattered tail wags over the low-growing gray-blue plant. Izzy rushes forward to chase him and hits the hill flat-backed. His nose is out in front, angling through the cactus. It feels like everything is watching us.

The chase leaves us empty. We roll downward into a north-pointing arm of the arroyo and return to a walk, then head up a low incline at a lope. The tracks of ravens and crows hop around a snag of juniper where last year's runoff grabs a pocket of apache plum and makes a bed for desert mice and rabbit. Their little batting triplets of toes, like eyelashes, jump into sequence as we run past them. Izzy feels like a racehorse, churning in the soft sand. The arroyo bends hard to the left and Izzy does a flying change to balance himself. His hindquarters grab like surefooted elk. My hips circle his back. Up. Down. Around and through.

I don't often feel as if I belong. People have never been easy for me. What I see on the outside—their gestures, the way they walk, how they hold their heads—doesn't match the words coming from their mouths. I'm not the girl who never leaves the corner at the party. I'm the girl who doesn't go to the party in the first place. When I'm with Flor and Sarah, Rex and Paul, even Randy—I know I belong. All our troubles, all our inadequacies, we wear them on the outside. There are no perfect, pretty people at the ranch. We are the ugly, the difficult, the invisible, the broken. Nothing is hidden. It is why horses have always been easy for me. They're honest. They show me exactly how they feel. How could the livestock team do this? The lies, the sneaking, the hiding? How could they lie about something I thought was so real? How could they tear it apart?

I turn Izzy hard left, and we scramble up the rim of a barranca. I hear screeching from above. Two red-tailed hawks circle with magpies chasing from behind. The hawks scream and flutter their wings, trying to keep the magpies off their backs. The rim is narrow, dropping steeply on both sides. I feel my butt cheeks squeeze together, trying to make myself feel thinner. I can hear rocks and dirt falling behind Izzy's hooves, cascading down the embankment.

There must have been a plan. Two months ago, Omar told me they lost the key to the tack room and hay barn. We couldn't ride that day. They went to town with Daniel and made a copy from the original. Was it a lie? Did they steal the key? Is that how they got the box in and out of the hay barn? Paul and James also went down to southern New Mexico for Paul's brother's funeral, about the same time the key went missing. I know Paul's family are all dealers. The whole family has been in and out of prison, including his niece and nephews in juvenile detention. It's a family tradition, he told me one Sunday after breakfast.

"It goes like this," he said to me as he squeaked his chair closer to the dining room table and leaned toward me. "I'm in for one year, then parole. When I'm out, usually my brother and sister are in. Whoever is out keeps the business going." His mom and dad overdosed and died when he was fifteen. He never went to high school. The siblings inherited the business, which ran from their double-wide trailer, night and day, every day of the week.

When Paul was in prison, he taught himself to read. As his reading improved, he began to teach other men over lunch or at recess. The guards became suspicious over these secret meetings.

Fights broke out and Paul was put in solitary confinement. He lived in an eight-by-eight-foot cement-block room, scratching days into the walls and waiting for the fifteen minutes he had each afternoon to walk out into his cage. The cage was even smaller than his room. It was a four-by-four-foot wire-fenced box, completely contained. There was nothing in the cage. No bench to sit on. No other men to talk with nearby. Its only advantage was sunlight. Paul would stare up at the sky and speak to the birds that flew by, to the clouds, to the sun. It was the fifteen minutes in the cage, his fifteen minutes communing with the world, that motivated him to try and break the cycle of prison and drugs. He became desperate to live in the world again. He swore to himself he could do it. He wrote to the ranch for an interview. It took a year to get the interview. He waited another six months for the judge's recommendation. Almost two years went by before he was transferred here. Was it at his brother's funeral when they loaded his suitcase with drugs? Is that who brought the drugs onto the ranch?

My head is spinning stories, bits of memory splinter into my mind as my body rocks back and forth on top of Izzy, heading eastward and uphill toward the Sangre de Cristo Mountains. The Truchas Peaks now straight in front of us, deep snow on their western slopes and in the bowl between them. My home sits at the base of these mountains. Looking up at these two points on the southern end of the Rockies from my porch window every morning lets me know who and where I am. Juniper berries, piñon, and a few pines scent the air. Clouds are coming over the mountains from the eastern plains. I'll need to head back before the rain hits and the arroyo fills with floodwater.

There's lather poking a foamy head out from under the saddle pad resting on Izzy's shoulders. His gallop has slowed to a traveling lope. One ear is on me, the other pins itself to the landscape around us. The arroyo channel tightens, and the walls climb higher, until it feels like we are being shot through a portal. The light is smoky, and the sun no longer hits the top of our heads. I squint my eyes and bring the world down to a pinhole in front of me. I imagine riding through this bright white dot and out onto the other side. I feel we could ride into that tiny speck of light, weightless and free.

The reins dangle from Izzy's neck, and I begin to close my eyes. He slams to a halt, and I land forward on his neck. Three young bucks blend into a tall pile of brush right in front of us, sipping from a pool of water left over from last night's rain. Izzy holds his head high, watching the animals carefully. The first buck is older; he has three points on each antler. The other two have fuzzy bumps barely visible poking up beside their ears. The middle buck lifts his head and licks at the moisture dripping from the long hairs around his muzzle. He stares at Izzy as he would a brother, deer and horse one and the same. He doesn't see me, smell me, or care about me. He dips his head back down and keeps drinking. The sucking of their tongues sounds like children drinking from a water fountain.

Maybe it wasn't that I missed something, some clue that I should have noticed. Maybe I saw everything perfectly. I saw my students for who they are, not who they used to be. I saw their hope, their hard work, their sorrow. Over the last year, they have carved away at their past and sculpted a partial return, perhaps to the people they were before all the trouble began. Maybe I just saw them like the young buck sees Izzy. Something that seems to belong in this world. The way Paul felt when he started speaking with the birds.

The big buck turns and walks east up the arroyo. The two

smaller ones follow close behind. Izzy watches them leave with
keen interest. He drops his head and licks his lips. I jump off and
take him over to the watering hole. His hooves sink into the
tracks left by the deer. I look down at my own boot marks beside
theirs, then reach for the water bottle in my saddlebag and take
a long swallow.

I DON'T CHECK IN at the dining-hall desk two days later. I don't
check in, like I usually do, to see who is scheduled to be down at
the barn. It has been more than forty-eight hours since we found
the box. I haven't been sleeping well. I tossed around in my bed-
sheets half-awake until three in the morning. At seven o'clock
my phone rang. It was Janet, my farrier, wanting to know when
we could schedule our next appointment to shoe Izzy. Janet is a
recovering drug addict, thirteen years sober. She had warned me
about addicts, how high the chances were for failure. I let her
know about the box, how I was heading over to the ranch but
didn't know who would still be there.

"We're not all going to make it, Ginger. You understand that,
right?" she questioned me, reiterating a harsh truth she's told me
before.

Of course, I know that. I know the path to recovery is a
crooked line. Learning how to fall and get back up is the skill
this ranch tries to instill in all the residents. The mistake I made,
my ultimate failure, was to think what I had with the livestock
team was permanent. That nothing could touch it. I should have
known better.

"Sounds like you'll have fewer friends over there today, Ginger," Janet said. I know she will hold the hard line. Janet has told
me more than once that if she fell back into drugs, she wouldn't

live to see sober again. She knows something I do not. Something I will never know.

"Next Tuesday is good for me if you can make it." I changed the subject, and we scheduled our appointment.

"They are lucky to have you. I hope they know it," she told me as we said goodbye.

I DRIVE THROUGH the metal gate, scanning the property for familiar faces. My eyes and the flesh around them are puffy from crying in my truck. I wave toward the residents working in the woodshop where Paul and Rex should be. I wave again to the men in the automotive shop where Omar, Tony, and Randy work. I pass the ceramic studio. Sarah runs the ceramic shop. I see no one in the studio. The doors are wide open, showing the empty chairs surrounding the workstation. Worry sinks further down my body.

When I turn north toward the corrals, I can see the horses all gathered and tied to the pipe corral railing, but no sign of the residents. As I get closer, Tony and Randy come out from the tack shed and stand ready to greet me. Randy has a greasy mechanic's hat on with his large hands crammed into the pockets of his baggy jeans. Tony is the picture of control, standing tall and alert, watching me pull down the drive, in slow motion. He opens the driver-side door of my truck as I turn off the ignition. I step out and am greeted with a long embrace. It isn't a hug exactly. It feels more like he's hugging me to hold me up. Randy stands back a short distance and can't look at us.

"Is this it? Is this all that's left?" I ask them.

"Eliza is still here. She's waiting for you to arrive. They won't let her come down here by herself," Randy tells me.

Eliza walks around the corner of the women's dorm. Without Flor. Without Sarah. They are gone, along with Paul, Rex, and Omar.

I turn toward Eliza and bend over, holding my wet face in my hands. Eliza grabs me and picks me up. She holds me in the middle of her strong body for so long it feels like I am dissolving into her muscles.

"Where are they?" I whisper into her ear.

She shakes her head. *No.*

"I can't," she says. "I'm not allowed to talk about it."

Whenever anyone is asked to leave the ranch, the rule is no one can talk.

"Come on." Tony puts his arm around my shoulder. "Let's get the horses saddled. We need to go for a ride."

CUT ME OUT

February / 2014

The arroyos are flash flooding on my way home. They bubble and churn through the culverts under the highway, the water heading west to the Rio Grande. Branches of juniper, a baby's diaper, the cushion from a sofa flush by, as I drive north heading into an ever-darkening sky. Two to three times a year we get torrential rains like these. My cell phone buzzes with weather warnings, and I'm grateful I remembered to put my dogs inside before I left the house.

At the gate, I see my horses pacing in their corral, six inches deep with mud and floodwater. When it rains this hard, the mesa behind our house sends a monsoon of water into our low-lying corral. Moo lets out a scream when I open the truck door, which sends Izzy and my youngest horse, Ra, sliding and bucking around their pen. I pull through the driveway while Moo stands close to the fence, staring at me. His pawing splatters sludge all over his chest and belly.

I run to the house to get my raincoat and muck boots off the porch. My dogs wag their tails but don't get up. I wade through the ocher-colored water toward the farthest gate where the halters and lead ropes are tied. Ra runs into the horse shelter as I splash by. He crams himself into the corner like he always does each morning and evening when I come out to feed. Ra is four years old and our least-broke horse. He came to us terrified of people; his entire body trembled when anyone approached him. His routine of running into corners and hiding always makes me sad, but today it reflects the mood.

I look around at the fences that contain my herd. Every day I love nothing more than to come out and feed them, groom them, get on their backs and ride them. Today I see this swamp-filled corral, measured by fences and corners, this metal container of manure mixed with rock, sand, and slurry, and I wonder how in the hell could I ever feel good about this. Izzy pushes his hind legs out behind him, straightens his hocks, and takes a long yellow-red pee. It pours into this waterlogged mess and swirls around my legs.

Daniel and James met me at the gate late this afternoon. They were checking in to see if I was okay. I wasn't. I couldn't hide it. My face was so swollen from crying I could see my own puffy cheeks when I looked down. James leaned through the window on the driver's side, and Daniel's head tilted in the opposite window. They both looked as if they hadn't seen the sun in weeks.

"There wasn't much else we could do, Ginger," James informed me. "None of them came clean. No one would rat on the other."

"They were on the bench for two days, and no one said a

word," Daniel said, his face void of expression. "They were a team, and they went down like a team."

When pinned into a corner, two dogs will usually fight, I thought to myself. But what did I know about any of this? What did I know about the livestock team? Not much. Not much at all it seemed.

"Not even Sarah?" I asked them, hoping they would give me a hint that she tried to save herself.

"Not a word. She never said a word."

My attention snaps back to the clatter Moo is making as he paws at the metal gate that leads toward the pasture. Izzy is walking the fence line pacing and turning. His neck swings like a saw. *Cut me out.*

I think about walking into a place I could never leave, like this pen where my horses live. I would learn every inch of this space. I'd smell my own piss over and over, tug at my manure for meaning. I'd lean and chew on the fence posts, putting splinters in my gums. I would pace the line with dull, witless eyes, barely lifting my hooves off the ground as I wove, back and forth, in a corral so small I couldn't see when the rain was coming. I wouldn't remember the scent of sagebrush and meadow; instead I'd smell this stink of manure, and urine, and sweat that surrounds me.

Sheets of rain come pouring from the sky; I can see it land like walls around me. Visibility is low. Moo bangs on the gate three times with his hooves, then snakes his neck and tosses his mane. He wants out. I'm taking too long.

Today I'm grateful for the pasture we bought from our neighbors ten years ago. It's a small pasture that sits above the floodplain across the road from our house. Three acres of irrigated grassland that run alongside the Rio Grande. It cost more than most people pay for a home. Irrigated land is expensive and hard to find in the desert west. Glenda and I have worked multiple jobs for years to pay it off. We water the grasses on the one day a week we're not working.

Ra is still stuffed into the corner of the shed when I pass him carrying the halter, sliding downhill toward Moo. I lay the halter over Moo's neck, not even bothering to pull it over his head. I back him up as I open the gate inward. His hooves *ker-plunk, ker-plunk* through the muddy water, splashing sludge into my muck boots. My socks fill with goo.

Containment casts a spell over a body. Ra was chased by two men into the corners of his paddock for the first three years of his life. Whipping their ropes at his hindquarters, they would jam Ra's terrified body as far into the pipe corral corner as they could squeeze him. He tried to escape, jerking away from one corner and galloping straight into the next, where the men would lash at him again until he gave up. Until he stood shivering and motionless, screaming through his eyes. Some bodies will never be truly free.

I take Moo out the gate and cross the road checking for cars, but no one is out in this weather. Izzy tucks himself behind Moo's rump, while Ra splashes by and flies out in front. Moo pins his ears in irritation. Ra romps ahead of us, running into the pasture, tossing his front legs high into the air. I release Moo, and Izzy follows him into the field. I shut the gate behind them. The two of them lope across the pasture toward the bosque, the forest of trees growing alongside the river that protects the horses from wind, rain, and snow in the winter.

Ra finishes his youthful dash and pulls up between Moo and Izzy. The three of them bend over and feed on the leftover grasses from last summer's pasture. Behind them, farther to the west, I hear more calls of thunder and see the strikes of lightning hit the Jemez Mountains. The horses will move into the bosque if another storm comes in. They can take care of themselves now.

That night, I lie in bed unable to sleep. Glenda slumbers next to me, already two hours into a good night's rest. I roll from side to side, every ten minutes, taking a deep breath and trying to let go of the tension in my legs. I close my eyes and see Flor in the dining hall, talking to the newly arrived women. She sits across the table and speaks with calm, clear, deliberate words. She encourages them to take it one day at a time. She speaks about trusting their mentors and letting the system of the ranch change them from the inside. I've heard her give this talk many times. I know she believed it. She was certain of the new Flor. She thought her change was finished, finalized. But all she had was a foundation, with no house to put on top. I cover my face with pillows to quiet my tears.

Flor isn't finished with her prison term. The ranch will have called her parole officer to let them know that she has been kicked off the ranch. She is required to turn herself in if she ever leaves the ranch. Will she go and hide out at her mother's house? Will they pass the time on the sofa, talking about her brother, her aunt, how her dogs are doing? How long before she tells anyone the truth, that she's heading back to prison?

I roll over again, now facing Glenda. I can hear her quiet breath. I see her chest rise and fall with the moonlight. I begin to count with her breathing: one . . . two . . . ten . . . twenty-four . . . I fall asleep with tears crusting my eyes.

In the middle of the night, I am startled awake by the sound of voices carrying up our country road. Three men, obviously drunk or stoned, are shouting and laughing. They stop just outside the south gate of our property and start bantering back and forth. One man's demanding a smoke. Another man can't find his wallet.

Naked, I sit up, slide the blankets off, and walk out of the bedroom, onto our glassed-in porch. I see the men sitting on the black boulders we placed out in front of our fence, to keep the drunk drivers from flying around the curve in the road and careening into our front yard. They are passing a bottle between them. I poke my head out the storm door.

"Hey, guys, move along. We're trying to sleep," I shout loud enough so they can hear me. The dogs come to the open window and start to growl. The moon is up behind the men, and I can see their silhouettes rise and turn to face me.

"Fuck you. You fuckin' bitch," one of the men stutters. His words slur together. Glenda rattles out of a deep sleep and calls from the bedroom, "What's going on?" The dogs start barking.

"Get out of here, or I'll call the police," I say. The men laugh at me and keep passing the bottle.

"What the fuck you gonna do about it?" one of the men garbles.

I shut the storm door. Pissed, I rush through the hallway, back to the bedroom closet, and pull my gun out from under my winter sweaters. Still naked, I unlatch the safety on my handgun and step out the porch door, onto the wet cement stoop. I turn and face the sound of the men.

"What are you doing?" Glenda calls again.

I widen my stance, grab my right wrist with my left hand, and take a firm grip on the gun. I raise the loaded weapon over my head and point it straight at the sky. I suck in air through my nose. My lips are locked shut. My tongue shoves against the roof of my mouth. I fire off five bullets into the night sky. The ricochet of the gun jams my elbows down into my shoulders. The muscles on my neck turn to bone.

"Go! Go!" the men shout at each other. I can hear their sneakers slap against the pavement and see the vague outline of their bodies tracking south, down our country road. Their arms and legs pump and swing, pump and swing. Their torsos stumble and fall forward, picking themselves up just before they hit the pavement. I lose sight of them as they race around the curve of our road. I'm still holding the gun over my head.

"Get in here," Glenda grabs me off the stoop and pulls me onto the porch. "What is wrong with you?" She looks like she can't recognize me, standing there with the smell of a fired pistol in my hand. "Did you know them? Who was that?"

The adrenaline is leaving my body, and I can barely stand up. My arms go numb and start to shudder, with the gun vibrating in my hand. I taste the salt of tears leaking into the corners of my lips.

"I don't know. I don't know who they were." I lay the gun on the porch floor. The dogs come over and start sniffing it. I can't stand anymore. I'm light-headed. My skin prickles over my shoulders and neck. I sit down on the cold porch and the dogs start licking my arm. I place my head between my legs to calm the dizziness.

Glenda picks the gun off the floor and clicks on the safety. She goes into the living room and places it on the ledge just above the fireplace. I see her bare feet come back onto the porch and stand next to me. She bends over and wraps her warm body all around me.

"They're gone, right? They're gone?" I keep repeating.

"They're gone, Ginger," she says in a quiet voice. "Come on, let's get back to bed." I feel like a child next to her. I'm cold and trembling and falling apart. I can't see. I stub my toe into the rocking chair and wince forward. "Here, follow me," she says and leads me back to the bedroom where we lie together, faces to the ceiling, eyes wide open, the gunshots still ringing in our ears.

WALMART

March / 2014

It's Sunday and the parking lot is filled with work trucks and family vans. Near where I park, there's a young guy selling pit-bull pups out of a cage made to fit the bed of his Dodge Ram. Shopping carts are abandoned between cars, and the remains of empty plastic bags flap like pigeon wings against tires and light posts. This parking lot is always busy. An unarmed security guard drives past me in a silver Ford Focus. Sia booms from his speakers. *I'm gonna live like tomorrow doesn't exist. Like it doesn't exist.* His curly hair squiggles out from under his official company hat, and his face is covered in a full black beard and dark sunglasses. I wave to him as he passes.

I haven't been to the ranch for a few weeks. I can't make myself go back. I haven't called, either. I've busied myself at the other two ranches where I work, and today I need to shop for a week's supply of food. There are clouds coming down from the mountains, covering the sun and spreading a dull, gray light across the valley.

They were dropped here in this parking lot, I was finally told. They were given one phone call. They could call family, they could call friends, or they could call their parole officers. Each was driven off the ranch, one by one, and left here in the parking lot of Walmart. Left alone to wait for whomever they had asked to pick them up. By law, Flor, Sarah, Omar, and Paul were all required to call their parole officer. If they didn't, that would be considered breaking parole. The ranch is also required to notify the police once someone is asked to leave. Everyone, except Rex, had two choices: go back to prison or be on the run.

Maybe they begged for money while they waited. In their clean clothes, with their hair nicely cut and styled, looking nothing like addicts, they could have fooled a few people. They have learned to be gracious and greet people in the eye when speaking. They have learned how to listen and form a conversation full of interesting sentences. I imagine some of them were shaking. Sarah could have been crying, she had nowhere to go. I wonder if Flor was solid. She looked and acted like a person in full recovery, yet she was still a lying, sneaking drug addict who just had better cover now. Rex, tall and handsome with a beautiful smile, most likely waited for his father to drive up from Albuquerque. I hope he didn't call his friends from the street—homeless boys who could have rallied and found a car somehow. I'm almost sure Paul called his sister and brother, or someone in his family. Being in trouble was a way of life for Paul. Something he could always rely on. Or maybe some of them did call their parole officer. I prayed Omar made that call. He is young, insecure, and fully impressionable. He followed the livestock team into this trouble and will follow others like them into more if he doesn't have supervision.

I imagine Sarah wanted to call me. She knew my number by heart. She also knew the call would have been wasted. I could never go pick her up and save her from herself. I think she knew that much. Out of all the residents, Sarah broke my heart the most. There were times when I could see her as the young, happy Sarah. The way she must have looked before the pain. There were days when her skin would lie tender over her face without sags or wrinkles. Her hair draped down to her shoulders. Untangled, pure, straight hair that looked like a soft breeze waving around her. I remember seeing this carefree Sarah when she rode Scout through the obstacle course, knocking most of the obstacles over, laughing and falling forward, wrapping her arms around Scout's neck in a giant hug.

Over breakfast, with our plates full of pancakes, we told each other childhood stories. How my mother made me try out for cheerleading and how on the day of the tryouts I wiped out on my skateboard right in front of all the pretty, perfect girls. My knees were shredded and pocked with road pebbles, bleeding so much I couldn't perform my routine. Sarah told me she had a younger sister she would dress for school every day because her mother was drunk, or stoned, or gone. She searched the night before for the matching components: light-blue socks, pink ribbons for her sister's hair, miniature floral print dresses. She'd lay each item out carefully on the edge of their shared bed in preparation for the morning routine. Sarah often cried while she told me stories about her sister—a sister she hasn't seen in over fifteen years.

Walking into the fluorescent lights of Walmart, I realize I have no idea whom Sarah called to pick her up. She had no family nearby, and no one would have come even if they were close. Her father, her sister, her own children had given up on her. Sarah came to the ranch from a prison in Texas. She was alone and an outsider, and I would most likely never see her again. I don't know where to put the memories of her.

A woman dressed in Walmart blues with a round smiley face pasted on her chest rolls a shopping cart toward me and I thank her. She's frail and hunched over, but her eyes meet mine and we share a smile. I want to ask her how she is. Can I get her anything? It feels like she should be in the waiting room of a doctor's office, not standing here in these bright lights.

Shopping carts full of plastic toys, cheap clothes, gallons of milk and doughnuts, frozen lasagna, and sixteen-inch pizzas, pounds of hamburger meat, bags of avocados, and burlap sacks full of green chiles crowd the aisles. There are so many shoppers, every space feels narrow and tight, like my skin after a bad sunburn. Children swarm around their parents' carts, screaming for a toy or fighting with a sibling. Mothers' faces sag with fatigue and annoyance, pushing their overloaded carts along at a snail's pace, scanning the shelves for necessary items. My cart is empty, as I hike up one aisle, turn right, then right again, and head down the next.

An older woman stands in the middle of the next row, studying the fresh tortillas on the bottom shelf. Her daughter holds her up by the elbow. I try to slide my cart past them, but instead I bump their cart and push it farther into the aisle.

"I'm sorry," I apologize and try to roll their cart back into place. The mother and daughter turn away from the tortillas and look down at my empty cart.

"You'd better start putting something in there, my dear," the mother says with a smile. "Here, have some fresh tortillas." Her daughter takes the tortillas from her mother and hands them to me. "I used to make my own, every day, you know?" the mother tells me. I reach out for the plastic bag filled with fifteen plump tortillas.

"I'm always debating on which I like best, the thin ones or the nice soft ones, like these," I confess to the mother, who looks serious now, ready to give me a lecture on how to make the best tortilla. I can see a few buttons are missing at the top of her blue dress. The folds of skin under her chin lap down to form a U shape right above her bustline.

"Both," her daughter says. "Both are good." The three of us nod our heads in agreement and begin to roll our carts in different directions. Halfway down the grocery aisle, I realize that those are the first words I've spoken all day.

We are rolling our carts through this box store, right to left, left to right. It feels like we are taking part in a practiced military drill formation. I wish there was a bench somewhere along the meat and cheese section, or over by the produce, where I could sit and watch, like city people do on Sundays at the park. I need to shop, but what I need more is to sit and talk. I want to be with people who are going about their everyday business of being alive. I pull my cart to the side, bend over, and pick up a bag of pinto beans to go with my tortillas. When I look up, I see a crowd gathering down by the corn bin.

I roll my cart toward the sign that reads *California Corn* and start picking up the cobs like the rest of the shoppers. Two men, one in bib overalls with a neatly pressed white undershirt taut over his chest and another man dressed top to bottom in camouflage, are picking up the cobs and peeling back the layers to check for freshness and color.

"I like the white; the white is sweeter. Qué no?" The first man leans into the bin and picks up another piece of corn.

"Sí vecino, el blanco is the best corn of the summer," the camouflage man says, putting two cobs in his cart.

I peel back the husk of three corncobs to reveal an abundance of white kernels. The men smile at me with their dark, lumpy faces.

"Eeeeh. You won the prize, mi hija," the first man says to me and grins so wide I can see all the fillings in his back teeth. It doesn't take much to break me wide open. A few great pieces of corn. A man three times my size cheering me on.

"Thank you." I beam a smile back at him.

"Take more," the other man offers. "They're so fresh. They'll be gone by the end of the day." I pull out three more cobs and peel back the husks again.

My cart is starting to look a little better and so am I. I feel color coming into my face. I'm not so tired, and I feel I could push this cart around the store for a few more hours.

In the next aisle over, two adolescent girls are standing in the middle of the tomato section. I make my way over to browse through the choices. My eyes roam until I see the sign for *Local Tomatoes: Alcalde, New Mexico*. They are hydroponically grown just across the river from our house, and the price is good. I pick three irregularly sized, imperfect, fresh tomatoes and put them in the child seat of my cart. They roll around loosely, like squirming toddlers. When I look up, the girls are watching me. They scan my clothing, my shoes. I'm dressed like a guy in my denim workshirt and belted jeans. I'm obviously a woman with my long blonde hair pulled back into a ponytailed knot behind my head. I'm an older woman, likely the age of their mothers, who doesn't fit the norm for who and what a woman should look like. I smile at them, but they don't smile back. They walk away, bumping into each other's hips, whispering back and forth.

On my way to check out, I pass a worker loading California peaches into a giant box. He holds one up to show me. "Fresh today," he says. A young father cuts one open with his pocket knife and feeds it to the baby girl bobbing in his arms. The child gums at the peach pulp that spills out of her rubbery lips as the father tries to take his bandana out of his back pocket to wipe the baby's drool off her chin. The bandana falls to the ground right by my feet. I pick it up and hand it to the father.

"She's beautiful," I tell him, "and she loves these peaches, doesn't she?" I ask.

"She does. She likes any kind of fruit," he says and thanks me as he takes the bandana from my hand.

I watch him wipe her chin, her nose, her neck. The peach juice is dripping down the snaps of her jumpsuit. "What's her name?"

"Marie," he says.

"My grandmother's name," I tell him as we both stare at the baby, whose eyes blink open and closed, lost in the reverie of her peaches.

There are five people ahead of me in the checkout line, and everyone looks tired. Standing in the checkout line at Walmart, fatigue often catches up with me. Usually I stand with a slight quiver as I wait to be checked through, but today I feel better. The woman in front of me tells me how she finally got a job up in Los Alamos, and the older woman in front of her congratulates her.

"Aheeeh, mi hija, that's good. Good for you."

The man behind me is worried about his ice-cream cake melting. He's on his way to a birthday party, and everyone lets him move ahead in our line, so he can be on his way with his frozen cake intact. Eventually another woman with a smiley face on her chest rings my items up, and I roll out the automatic doors into a beautiful blue-sky day. The clouds have burned off, and the air feels fresh and cool.

I park my cart and carry the two bags of groceries uphill to my truck. I see a young woman about five feet back hustling to catch up to me.

"Excuse me, miss?" She's just behind me now, so I turn to face her. "We've run out of gas and are trying to get to Taos. Could you help us out?"

She's stringy and pale with torn jeans so long the tattered hem drags along the damp pavement and darkens the fabric above her worn-out high tops.

"Where's your car?" I ask, and she waves vaguely toward the northeast corner of the lot.

I look for the worst beater out there and see three guys in a Chevy Duster with its hood crunched in. The windows are rolled down and smoke seems to be exploding from the interior of the car. Tattooed arms hang out the windows. Their bald, shiny heads shimmer through the windshield. I have some cash in my wallet. Not much, but enough to get them some gas and be on their way, if that's how they'll spend it. Flor told me she used to work this parking lot before she came to the ranch. White women were the easiest to get money out of, she told me. In one afternoon, she could get enough cash for a few days' supply of heroin. I hesitate to answer the woman. Perhaps a few bucks will keep her from breaking into someone's car. Perhaps a few bucks will give her the chance to buy cleaner heroin, something not laced with that which could kill her. She's not interested in getting gas or food; that much is obvious. Skin hangs from her collarbone—no fat, no muscle. Her black hair falls forward across her gray cheeks. She watches me thumb through my wallet, with eyes that wink shut for far too long. I wonder whose daughter she might be.

We all come from somewhere. From broken homes. From

good homes. From rich families. Poor families. Foster care and adoption families. We all have origin stories. It's the one thing we all have in common.

I give the woman five dollars. She walks away without a thank-you. I see her wave at the Duster to come get her. The muffler sounds like a low-flying helicopter, black smoke pumps out from the back bumper. The men drive up to her and she jumps through the back door. They head out the lot, uphill past Wendy's, then up to the light where they turn south, back into Española.

Sitting inside the cab of my truck, I watch the shoppers come and go. Everyone in a hurry. Everyone with so much to do, so much on their minds. I'll busy myself, too. Go home and cook a meal for Glenda and myself. Tomorrow I'll head to work, riding horses all day at a ranch up north. I'll keep myself busy. I'll stay on track. I'll try not to let my mind wander to things I can't change.

I sit in the parking lot another fifteen minutes. Can't get myself to turn the key.

HUNDREDS MORE

March / 2014

"Ginger, are you there? Hello?" I recognize the voice at the other end of my cell, but I'm not answering. I put the phone down to my lap, bring it back to my ear, then back to my lap. I turn my truck north onto Highway 84, heading toward another horse ranch in Abiquiu. I'm already fifteen minutes late, and I still need to stop for diesel.

Shit, I say to myself and pull over.

"Ginger, it's Eliza. I'm calling to see if you're coming back." I shake my head *no* even though she can't see me, and I listen to her talk. Her voice is beautiful in my ear. I can see her smile, her fresh skin, the clarity in her eyes. I have watched Eliza change from a sullen, silent, hunched-over creature into a brave, insightful, generous woman over the last year. I'd like to believe in this voice at the other end of the line, but I don't know if I can.

"We've got two new people signed up for livestock," she says. "Everyone wants to know, when are you coming back?"

It's been over three weeks since I've been to the ranch.

Three eighteen-wheelers speed past me and rock my truck side to side. I roll my windows up and turn the air conditioner to low.

"I don't know," I tell her honestly. "What can I do that may help anyone there?" I fiddle with my windshield wipers, spraying the windshield three times to knock off the bugs. I bite my nails and wiggle my knees under the steering wheel, nervously. My clients in Abiquiu are texting, wondering when I'll arrive.

I teach every day. I ride horses six days a week. But right now the work lacks meaning. My clients are wonderful, caring individuals who love their horses. Most of them work long hours at their jobs and, with what free time they have, they devote themselves to their animals. I've always felt honored they put their trust in me. It is not the horses, nor is it my clients who leave me with this vacant feeling. It's stuck somewhere deep inside me—a hollow spot I've always known was there.

I don't fit neatly into this world. As a woman who loves women, I was born with the man my culture says I need, already a strong living presence inside my body. I am like other women, but I am nothing like them at all. Some days I'm filled with anger, some days nothing but sorrow. Some days I feel safe. But it is rare when I find a place where I feel I really belong.

I think about going back to the ranch and working with the residents again. Heartbreak and joy twist and compete, eventually dropping into my gut simultaneously. I feel queasy.

"Ginger, there will always be more of us. Hundreds more. Who knows what will be the thing that saves us? The horses, they saved me." Eliza speaks slow and deliberate, her tone measured and serious. She takes a long breath, then there is silence.

"Two new people? You have two new people on livestock?" I ask her.

Olivia and Joey—they want to join livestock—Eliza tells me. They are learning how to groom the horses and where to put the saddle. They're excited for me to return and teach them how to ride. It seems no one has missed a beat. One day follows the next. No one has given up. I'm the only one holding onto failure. I think about Terry, that feisty little filly, all those years ago. She never gave up, never gave in. Even after her injury, how she fought the famous trainer out the back of that big rig.

"Two new people," I say again. "That's great. Do they know anything about horses?" I ask Eliza.

"No, but we are teaching them what we know. Tony, Randy, and myself, we've been meeting every Tuesday and Thursday since you left."

They had gotten up the next day and stayed with the plan, working the horses, training new people. I went back to my busy life, my clients and horses, essentially running away from the one place I feel the most at home.

They keep working. They have too much at stake, too much to lose. *What do I have to lose?* I ask myself as I listen to a second round of silence at the end of my cell phone.

Everything. I have everything to lose.

"Ginger, we need you," Eliza says into my ear.

"I need you, too."

I insert the Bluetooth in my ear and pull back onto the highway.

"I can come out next Tuesday if that works. I'll bring my extra saddle and Moo, too." Two new people. Two new people. I wonder what they look like. The shape and gesture of their bodies. I wonder what the horses think of them.

OLIVIA

April / 2014

Shoulder to shoulder, we bend over to pick up Hawk's right front hoof. Olivia's hair drapes over her cheeks and hides her eyes from my view. She holds the hoof pick upside down. I turn it in her palm and feel her pull away from my touch. She's been on the ranch four months. She's eighteen years old. She's been in and out of juvenile and county detention centers since she was twelve. She gets out of jail, she goes back. In between these stints, she shuffles between foster homes.

She drops the hoof pick to the ground, straightens her back, and stands up. Her hands start shaking and flapping at her wrists. I step back from her and watch her eyes dart inside their white perimeter.

"I don't want to do this," she says as she keeps wringing her hands in circles, raising them to her ears like they have something to say.

"Do what?" I ask her, looking for clarification.

"Touch him. Touch Hawk. I don't want to touch him."

Eliza told me that Olivia has obsessive behaviors. She constantly wipes clean the doorknobs in the room she shares with two other women. She's worried people are touching her toothbrush, her soap and shampoo. At dinner, her fork, knife, and spoon can never touch her plate. If they do, she asks for a new set. Eliza thought having her out here with the horses could help.

I put my two hands out in front of me, palms up facing her. "Try it with me first."

"What?" she asks.

"Touch me. Lay your palm on mine and touch me."

Her thin, black eyebrows scrunch and thicken. Her turquoise-blue eyes close to a slit, and her lips wrinkle in disgust.

"You're going to have to touch someone, something that's alive, at some point," I tell her. "Come on, touch me."

She takes her hands up to her mouth and blows on them. She sighs through her open fingers, then moves her palms down. I feel the heat from their surface as she inches toward me and touches down like paper in the wind.

"That's it. Stay here a little while," I encourage.

She can't meet my eye. She's looking at the ground with a blank, worried expression. Her neck and shoulders pinch and tilt forward. She looks like she is shrinking.

"Okay. Good," I say. She rips her hands from my palm and starts twirling her wrists up by her ears again.

I want to reach out and hold her. Hawk stands behind her twitchy, swirling hands and keeps a close watch. She looks like an injured moth, upside down on the pavement, waving its wings, trying to get upright.

"We'll do it again, a few more times," I tell her.

She says yes with a nervous nod of her head. She takes a deep sigh. I can tell she wants to do it, just a little. She's made it through the worst and it didn't kill her. She sets her palms against my skin. She looks straight at me. The corners of her mouth rise a tenth of an inch. I can see her teeth break through her lips.

We're not allowed to touch here. But every day since I returned, I reach out to hug every person on livestock. I ask them how they're doing. Are they having any troubles? What new things have they been learning? They hug me again, just before I leave, one at a time, and thank me for coming. I hold their bodies like treasured friends, because I know at any moment, I could lose one of them. The touch of our skin, our chests and necks, the feel of ribcage against forearms, helps stave off my loneliness. I've spent my whole life feeling like I was odd, queer, different. Alone. None of that is true now. None of it. It never was.

There will always be more of us, hundreds more.

I know the flow of people onto this ranch will never end. I know Olivia, Eliza, Tony—all of them—will be replaced by others one way or another. This ranch receives over one hundred calls from prison every few days. Only a handful will pass their interview and trial period. Olivia, Randy, the whole livestock team made it through. They are the winners, the ones who showed some promise. I know that at any given moment they will falter, make big mistakes, fail to be who they strive to be. I know now that my role isn't to save them; it's to help them get back up. These hugs are my way of saying, *I'm here and I want you to stay.*

I hug everyone, everyone except Olivia. She stands back from the group, close or behind the cottonwood tree, where she looks down at the ground as the procession of hugs continues. She says hello. She says goodbye. She thanks me for coming. But we never touch. Olivia never touches anyone.

"How about Hawk?" I ask after our third round of hand on hand. Hawk is standing in the shade with one of his hind legs cocked. He looks sleepy. "How about we try to put Hawk's hoof in your palm?" I ask her. She's not so sure. Her body folds forward, heading toward the fetal position. "I'll do it first. I'll show you. I'll be right here." Olivia comes along my shoulder and tucks behind me.

"Alright," she whispers.

I move in close to Hawk's shoulder, pinch behind his knee lightly, and he lifts his hoof off the ground and places it into my cupped hand. Olivia is peeking over my shoulder.

"Just let it rest here," I say to her. "Give him a nice round spot to cradle his hoof. You can use both hands if that feels better." Olivia cups her hands together in front of her waist and looks into their empty pocket. I place Hawk's hoof back on the ground as Olivia moves around in front of me and into position. Her fingertips rub together in a fit of nerves. Her legs wobble. Her torso is frozen in place. She lifts her arms and hides her hands behind her head.

"I can't," she says. "I can't." She shuts her eyes. "Greenhouse—I need the greenhouse," and she takes off at a fast walk toward the greenhouse, talking to herself in sentences that are incoherent. "We were here first. After dogs and the tile guy plumber man." I follow closely behind her, past the ceramic shop and commercial freezer, up toward the top of the property where the greenhouse sits. She opens the glass door and heads in, and I enter behind her. She places both her hands into the dark cultivated dirt and starts kneading the soil like a cat on a soft pillow.

Eliza runs in after us. She looks at me, then at Olivia. "It's okay," Eliza reassures me. "She runs in here sometimes. The dirt seems to help her." Olivia looks over at Eliza, nods her head, and keeps kneading.

"Olivia, talk to me. Tell me what you had for lunch." Eliza tries to bring her back.

"We had burritos, Eliza. Don't you remember?"

The dirt seems to help her.

When Moo was younger I taught him to lie down. He was shy and fearful of most things. Anything that came up behind him made him bolt. Lacking confidence isn't uncommon in young horses. As their experience grows, as they learn how to accept objects and movements in the world around them, they eventually become gentle and accepting. Still, at the age of seven, Moo was bolting and leaping sideways over the slightest sounds in the bushes. I had read that lying horses down to the earth calmed their nervous system. I learned how to take him to the soft ground of the round pen, in the cool morning air, and quietly lie him down in the warm sun. I'd put a rope over his neck, pick up one of his front legs, and rock him sideways. First his knee would buckle, then he would drop onto one shoulder and pause. He would let all his weight settle over to one side of his body and gently fall to the ground. He'd stretch his long neck over the sand and rest there for fifteen minutes or so as I caressed him all over his body. His breathing relaxed and slowed to such a pace he sounded as if he was snoring. Every few weeks during that year, I'd lie him down. That was twelve years ago.

"I've got an idea," I tell Eliza. "See if you can get Olivia back to the barn."

Moo is hot and sweaty from Randy's recent ride around the obstacle course when I return to the corrals. The timing couldn't be better. Moo will love a roll in the round pen dirt to dry himself off.

"Olivia's coming back," I tell Randy, following with a request to take off Moo's saddle and bridle, then tie him to my trailer.

Olivia has her hair pulled away from her face. Her cheeks are flushed. She and Eliza walk back to the barn without a care in the world.

"Are you feeling better, Olivia?" I hear Tony ask. The sound of his question makes me realize that everyone has seen Olivia duck into the greenhouse on multiple occasions.

"Yes, thank you," Olivia tells him and heads over to where Moo and I are standing by my horse trailer.

"Hey, Olivia, I'm going to try something. I hope you can trust me. I won't make you touch anyone, I promise."

I ask Eliza to take Olivia into the round pen and sit down in the four inches of deep sand over near the far rail. I bring Moo through the gate and take him to the center of the pen. He starts to paw the ground, telling me he'd like a good roll. I back him up and make him stand still. Olivia and Eliza are looking up at us from their low position on the ground. I take the rope over Moo's neck and pick up his left front leg. I rock him onto his right shoulder until he begins to fall off balance. It doesn't take long for him to buckle to his knees and rest sideways on his right shoulder. He lets out a long droning sigh, then falls over, flat onto his side.

"Holy cow!" Randy exclaims, then runs over and leans against the rail. Tony and Joey, the other new member of livestock besides Olivia, come up behind him.

I sit on the ground behind Moo's back and start scratching his withers with my fingernails. He rubs his neck back and forth against the sand in rhythm with my hand. Everyone is silent. Eliza and Olivia crawl through the sand on all fours and sit down behind my back. Moo's ribcage heaves and fills with air, then rests back down. A low rumbling groan of contentment leaves his mouth as I rub all over his body. Olivia sits so close to me that the side of her rump touches mine. I scooch over and she crawls right beside me, her knees touching Moo's back. My arms rise and fall with the rhythm of Moo's breath. I look to my side and meet Olivia's amazement.

She sits up on her knees with her arms out in front of her body, floating her hands just above Moo's ribcage. She rolls up the sleeves on her light blue hoodie. I look down at her right forearm where the scars tell stories of her battered childhood. Moo lets out another long groan.

"Touch him, Olivia," Randy whispers from the other side of the rail.

Olivia tips her head in Randy's direction. One thin tear drips down her cheek.

HIDDEN LANGUAGE

April / 2014

Language can be taken. It can be lost. Stolen. Severed. It is not a birthright. Not everyone is heard. Not everyone gets to make a sound.

Many of the people I have met at this ranch enter the program like zombies: pale, silent, ghosts of themselves. Their thoughts, their sentences, their ability to answer a question, have atrophied. Whether it was prison that silenced them, or foster homes, poverty, or rape—almost everyone I have met on this ranch struggles to find words, to speak, to share and communicate.

Over this past year, I have watched them shed their protective cocoons of silence. Eliza hardly muttered a word before she held Willie's hooves between her thighs. Randy could rarely speak the truth before Moo stood above his crumpled body and waited for him to get back up. Olivia hasn't needed the greenhouse since the day she met Moo. She speaks in lengthy, coherent paragraphs as she grooms the horses, touching their bodies with the softness of her palm. Tony is kind. He's not angry. He's no longer quick with his words. His hands rest at his side, without twitching or rubbing. Occasionally, I see him standing in the middle of a group of residents, his arms folded loosely across his chest. He is just standing there, listening, not saying a word.

The back of my throat hasn't burned in months. I have relied on the language of these ranch horses. I knew that if we could learn to listen to what their bodies were saying, then maybe they would learn to trust us. They remind me that listening is the first step towards speech.

I wasn't born without a language. I chose to listen to movement over words. I craved silence not sound. Speaking aloud was something I slowly grew into, first by reading books aloud in my room. Standing in front of the mirror, I would read the words over and over, watching how my mouth formed the sound.

At the age of six, I still refused to speak in public. Never raising my hand to answer the teachers at school. I could talk to my mother, and sometimes my sisters, but most of the time I hid in my room. Kindergarten, first, second, and third grade were discordant, a jangle of harsh repetitious noise.

During school recess, I would run to the far corner of the playground and lie in a tall pile of leaves. I'd sink down below the surface and watch the shimmer of sunlight filter through the patterned maple leaf. When the bell rang, and the schoolyard calls of boys and girls faded behind brick walls, I would shake the leaves off and rush back into the building, just before they locked the doors.

I'm still trying to find my language. At parties, over dinner with friends, I feel slow. While everyone rushes in with words and laughter, sometimes it's hard for me to keep up. I could chime in, but my words don't match the tactile sensation I feel on the inside. I struggle to say the things I can't feel. Maybe that is what suppresses so many voices: sensing that our words are empty shells.

Every word I speak on this ranch is necessary. Essential. I realize this now. What I say, how I say it, can make the difference in someone's life—big or small.

Yesterday Randy was saddling Estrella. She was unsettled and walking circles around him as he tried to cinch the saddle onto her back. I heard his frustration. His constant refrain of "whoa, whoa, Estrella" was getting her more excited. It wasn't just the words, but the sound, the frantic tone of his words that made her spin. Animals hear the vibration more than they hear the words themselves.

"It would be better if you said nothing at all," I spoke to Randy in a soft voice. He knew, as soon as I said those words, what change he had to make. Randy took in a long breath and let it out slow. He closed his eyes. He remained silent, his eyes opened, then he reached for Estrella's mane and began scratching her behind her ears. Estrella dropped her head and exhaled, the sound of it made Randy smile.

Randy has told me, over and over, how much working with the horses has helped him get along better with the residents on the ranch. When things get tough, when there are arguments and people lose their temper, he relies on the skills he has learned with the horses. For the first time in his life he has learned to calm his mind and use it as an asset inside his community.

Here on this ranch every word has meaning. Every pause, every moment of silence, every nuance of inflection; these can hold great consequence. It has taken a year for me to recognize that my voice, the words I speak, have the capacity to save lives.

BROKEN

April / 2014

Joey trembles as he greets me. As I reach out for his hand, the quivering of him races up my arm. His sentences are run-on, out-of-breath monologues. He tells me he has six months on the ranch, three years before that in prison, and two more to go to fulfill his term. He asks me if I think he can learn how to care for Luna.

Luna is not a beginner's horse. Mostly she trusts Tony and Randy, but even they have some difficult days with her. Luna is the one horse we still can't ride. She won't let us saddle her, and putting anything over the area where she broke her nose sends her into a tantrum. I know Joey feels a sense of closeness to her. He tells me this every day when I arrive. He's not alone in his desire to care for Luna, just about everyone wants to help her. Most of the time Luna's not interested.

"We need the help," I tell Joey. "We'll take it slow and see how it goes."

I show Joey the curry comb. It's a large, round metal comb with a wooden handle. The bottom ridges will scratch away the dust embedded in Luna's black-and-white coat. I place it in his hand, lay my hand on top of his, and start to groom. We make swirling circles across her chest, belly, topline. I stand behind him, close. Our bodies touch like dancers. We move along her curving spine, down to her rump, parallel with Luna's powerful body. Joey is just a few inches away from her. I can feel the rise and fall of his breath on my chest. I give him directions.

"Take your time, Joey," I encourage. "The one thing Luna likes is a good scratch."

Luna exhales and blows out through her nostrils. Tiny droplets of misty snot hit the pipe corral fencing and give a faint ring like a faraway bell. Joey stops for a moment. He checks Luna's eyes. They are shut. She is in that standing-up, resting place.

Joey sits at his desk, in front of the phone lines, every day. *Hello, this is the DS Ranch. Can I help you?* Under the desktop his legs bounce up and down, his heels tap in rapid fire. His head scans left to right, as he chews and snaps on a small piece of gum. The phone job is teaching him how to talk to people, to care about others. *Can you hold, please? I will get you that information.* He takes a long exhale after each call, audible sighs heard across the room. In between calls, he holds his breath and bites his nails.

Many of the people on this ranch started using drugs in high school and never graduated. Their addiction took over before most of them ever held a job. During the first six months on the ranch the residents focus on life skills. How to greet and speak with each other respectfully. How to dress in public. Basic hygiene protocols. Being on time for work. Joey hasn't made much progress. He tries but rarely meets my eye when he speaks. His hair is cut short but never combed. He dresses in baggy, over-sized clothes most days when he comes down to livestock. His parents abandoned him and all his younger siblings when he was twelve. He had no role models. No one to show him what the rules were and how to live by them.

Joey grabs a hairbrush and pulls on Luna's mane. He picks up the hair conditioner and works it into his palms. Spreads it, with his fingers, between the twisted knots tying up her long, white hair. He reminds me of a father readying a daughter for school. He works the knots out, one by one, holding down the roots with his other hand. He is worried he might be pulling too hard. Luna stands perfectly still. She cocks one leg and moves her mouth in a circle. Joey lifts her hooves. She bends her knee and flips her leg into the air, offers her body to him. He picks at the rocks and clay caked into the crevices. He inspects each hoof, then places them back down. He takes a soft brush from the grooming box and starts his deliberate journey across her body.

Joey has ulcers high up into his chest. He eats small meals, half a peanut-butter sandwich. Snacks on cookies all day. Carries their crumbles in his pockets. He is alone. His parents are gone to addiction. His siblings are either in jail or are using. He is illiterate even though he is in his late twenties. Eliza helps him with reading on Tuesday nights in the library. He wants to pass his GED. He would be the first in his family.

Joey leans against the top rail of the round pen as Tony takes Luna by the lead and places her in the round pen.

"Go ahead, get in there, you can do it," Tony encourages.

Joey shrugs his shoulders.

Luna roams around the pen. She's distracted. Alone. The rest of the horses are turned out to pasture.

"Go ahead. Jump in and work with her." Tony's trying to be helpful, but Joey doesn't budge.

Joey moves away. He walks over to the cottonwood tree, plants himself beside it, looking away from Luna. Tony shakes his head, then turns and heads off to get Hawk. I am over by the pipe corral fence trimming Willie's hooves. Bent over, I observe Joey from my upside-down view. His body has that downward slump that says he wants to fold into nothingness. His legs are spread, shoulders hunched, his head is tipped to the left. He looks like the eternally disappointed child. What he wants most is in that round pen, but he has no idea how to get it. Joey wants to be close to Luna, loose inside the pen, but he needs support.

Luna stares at Joey's back. She tries to smell between their bodies but can't grasp the scent. He is too far away. She waits for some movement. I can see she wants his body to turn, to move an inch, to show some sign of life. The emptiness of him confuses her. Ears pricked forward, chest pressing against the rails of the round pen, she is transfixed by Joey's disappearance, his body becoming a hollow shell.

Horses look for life in a body. Our outer shell is rigid, but on the inside we are like water, continually fluid. Animals feel the absence of that flow: the stagnation, the crippling death of no motion. Everything is movement to a horse. Everything has a current; the smallest ripple has so much to say. Luna stares across the short distance, watching a body that has no life.

I finish with Willie, put him back in his corral. Skirting past Joey, I can feel the brush of air between us and imagine he can, too. I know not to pull or push on him; I know this will only shut him down further.

Luna breaks her gaze from Joey and meets me by the round pen gate. She stands a few feet away. I wish she would move closer.

I raise my arm and reach out to scratch her neck. *Don't touch*, she pins her ears and backs away. Wanting anything from Luna sends her into retreat. I put my arm back down. She returns, just close enough to wave her nostrils in and out to take in my scent.

Joey pads across the dirt driveway and comes up behind me without a sound. I feel him on my back. He's waiting for me to notice him. *Why won't he speak?* He haunts me when he leaves his body like this. I want to shake him, rattle his shoulders, ask him what he needs. But I know better. I don't turn around. Luna shifts her feet, slants her body in his direction. Ears pushed forward. One blue eye, one brown eye, both are on him.

"I want to go inside the pen," Joey says.

"Do you want me to stay?" I ask.

"Yes."

Luna's half-broke. She lets us groom her mane and tail, clean her hooves and trim them. She allows Tony and Randy to halter her in her corral, but no one else. A few weeks back, when Tony was leading Luna into the round pen, she turned and swiftly kicked him on the side of his ribcage just above his hip and sent him skidding sideways. He was black-and-blue for over a week, but no broken ribs

"She's a hard one, just like us," Tony has said many times.

I'm not sure Luna will ever let down her guard. I've met a few other horses like her over the years. Horses who hold onto their sovereignty. They will never let their trainer take full control. It is a hard thing to learn how to do, to leave some power in the hands of the animal. I met a horse a lot like Luna in 2008 when I went to Raleigh, North Carolina, to teach a horsemanship clinic.

Her name was Coco, a young warmblood mare, six years old, whose owner was a fox hunter. There were twelve women in the clinic, and everyone wanted a private lesson. That meant I taught each rider privately, no one standing around watching. That wasn't true when Coco entered the arena. Her owner led her through the gate with a crowd of interested spectators following behind. Coco was already high on adrenaline. Her knees bounced off the arena footing like balloons, hopping and lifting her front legs into the air. She was saddled and bridled, with the reins not yet over her head. Her owner pulled on the reins, trying to keep Coco from leaping on top of her.

"Are you going to ride her first or am I?" her owner asked.

I laughed so hard that my microphone squealed. The crowd joined in the laughter. Coco's owner was confused. She had asked a serious question, the only one she knew to ask.

"Can someone bring me my rope halter and lunge rope, please?" I directed toward the crowd, then I went to work trying to keep Coco's feet on the ground. She seemed like a joyful mare when she first entered, but as soon as I asked her to put her left front leg there and her right hind leg here, her ears fired flat back, her lips peeled open, and she charged me with her teeth. I jumped to the side avoiding a strike and kept up my business of putting her hooves where I wanted them to be. It was clear why Coco had drawn a crowd. She wasn't going to give me anything for free.

I whistled, carefree, into the mic ignoring the hostile look on her face. I spun my lead rope around her flank, up toward her ribcage, near her shoulder. Each time asking her to put her hooves in a specific place, a thing so simple most horses agree and abide quite quickly. Not Coco. Those were her feet. Her only chance to protect her authority. They were her main tool for flight, for safety and food, and for all the other necessary things in a horse's life. No, I could not have her feet. If I was in front of her, she would lunge at me with her mouth. If I was behind or beside

her, she'd fire and try to land a kick. I worked her for almost two
hours each day until she attempted to give me at least half of what
I was asking.

By the third afternoon of the clinic, I had Coco standing still
to be mounted, jumping three-foot fences, and walking quietly
through a grassy field. Three things she had never done in her
life. Her owner was giddy with excitement over the progress.

"I still don't know how you did it," she said to me on our last day.

"I made a deal with her," I explained. "I told her where I
wanted her to go, then let her choose how fast she wished to get
there. I only took half of her freedom away."

JOEY CLIMBS THROUGH the rails of the round pen. He has his
white high-top sneakers on, black jeans two sizes too big with
a rope tied around the waistband, and a bright yellow hoodie
rolled over his head. Luna spins away when he enters and sets
herself against the opposite wall, parallel to Joey. I watch them
from outside the pen. The wind picks up a dust devil and spins
itself around us. Dust, manure, and small pebbles clink against the
rails. Luna startles. Joey, nothing. Not even the slightest flinch.
I close my eyes. The dust stuffs itself up my already dried-out
sinuses. I scratch away the dirt stuck inside the corner of my eyes
and wipe my lips clean of grit. When I open my eyes, Joey looks
like a stone.

I am going to wait. Not say a word. Joey will ask for what he
needs when he's ready. I know that about him now. Luna lengthens her neck toward the ground, it arches defiantly. She is not
interested in eating. She throws her left front hoof into the air,
smacks it onto the ground, and starts pawing. Is she mad? Does
she want him out of there? Snort. A gruff, blunt blow from Luna's
nostrils, and her neck straightens. Her head raises. She twists

toward Joey, expectant. She wants him to move. She wants him to be alive. She picks up her left hock and bends it underneath her body, turning her left hip off to the right. Perpendicular now to the rail, she faces Joey straight on. She has that worried look again. She's concerned about the lifeless man in front of her. She takes a step forward, right at him. They are thirty feet apart. Joey backs up; his butt hits the rail. He stumbles. Luna stops. He moved. He's alive.

"What does she want?" Joey asks.

"She wants you to move," I say.

Luna has on her purple-and-red halter. She has had it on for a little over a year. She won't let us take it off, and I decided maybe that was best. Who knows, if we take it off, we may never get it back on.

"Go somewhere. She doesn't know what you are. You have to move!"

Joey walks off to the left, staring at the ground. With his yellow hoodie and black pants, he looks like a giant yellow-headed blackbird inching his way around the pen. His white sneakers scuff to orange as he shuffles, not much bend to his knees. He drags his legs along like ancient walking sticks. Luna turns on her haunches. Her ears are darts that follow Joey around the pen. She is fine with Joey doing all the work. She pivots easily. Like a coach studying her player, critical and assessing each mechanical movement: his breath becoming short and fast, his right toe stubbing the dirt harder than his left, his left arm swinging half the distance of his right. As he passes me, I can see he feels ridiculous. He rolls his eyes up to his brow and pinches his lips downward. He wants to touch her, to hold the intimacy he feels when he grooms her. He wants her close, but if he advances, she will run. Her first instinct to flee from humans still works in her favor.

Joey looks up from under the hoodie. Three of his dormmates are cruising by, and it's obvious he feels embarrassed. He looks back down.

"Hey, E, what you doing dude, playing Ring Around the Rosie?" They laugh.

Joey doesn't look up. Says nothing. He's getting anxious. Holding his breath. Wagging his torso back and forth as he walks away from the guys. I can hear him mumbling under his breath. From around the corner, by the cottonwood tree, the ranch dogs come sprinting. Barking and chasing four wild kittens underneath the old chicken coop. Luna flies across the pen. Joey darts away from her. Tony and Randy run over and pull the dogs off. They take them back to the dining hall to pen them up. Joey walks up to the rail that faces the dilapidated coop, just a few feet away from the round pen, and calls for the kittens. We have been trying to catch them for weeks, their mother no longer around.

"Kitty, kitty," Joey sings.

He has forgotten all about Luna for a moment as he calls out to the kittens.

"Here, kitty, kitty."

I walk around the outside of the pen, close to the chicken coop. Luna takes a few steps toward Joey as he continues his song.

"Kitty, kitty, kitty."

The kittens come out from under the coop. Four black and one white with black socks. Luna has moved in closer to see them. She is about five feet behind Joey, with her neck pushed forward and her haunches bunched up underneath, ready to spring back in reverse if necessary. She takes a few last steps and settles alongside Joey's shoulder. She reaches her neck over the top rail and stretches down to touch the kittens. Joey turns his neck halfway. The corner of his eye meets hers. He turns back to the kittens.

They are curling their backs upward and scratching themselves on the fence posts down by his feet.

"Ginger, can you go get the cat carrier from the barn?" he asks me.

I head to the barn to find the carrier. It is stuck behind two dusty, old saddles. Heading back toward the round pen, I see the backside of Luna and Joey, standing right next to each other, staring down at the kittens.

Joey bends and reaches through the rail to pick up one of the kittens, who is rubbing his little arching back on his leg. Joey turns and walks across the pen toward me. I have the carrier in my arms. Luna walks behind him. Her nostrils are back to work. Poking her nose into Joey's arms, trying to get a good sniff. He hands me the kitten and chuckles. A sheepish grin covers his face as he turns and goes back for the other three kittens, with Luna in tow.

All four kittens are in the carrier: purring, scratching, and crying. Joey goes to the center of the pen and Luna follows. He takes his time. Turns and faces her. Reaches out to scratch her, and she stays. She drops her head. He removes his hoodie. He grooms her across the neck and up to her withers, using his nails to scratch the itch beneath her dirty coat.

His face opens to a smile. His back is straight. He moves his arms up and over Luna's body without hesitation, like he's done this all his life.

"Can I take her halter off?" Joey asks me.

I hesitate with surprise. *No, he can't take off the halter. We'll never get it back on*, I say to myself. Any time we move too fast toward Luna's face she shies and whips her head around, often knocking a resident backward and off their feet. I've been worried that one day she's going to really hurt someone. She has not forgotten her injury, guarding herself at all cost. Over the last year, we haven't come very far with Luna. Looking at her now, I wonder if this is the time to try something new. I don't want to rope her again. I look at Joey and Luna, standing as a pair now.

"Well, maybe. Unbuckle the halter, slide it off her nose—only partway—then put it back on. I want to see how she'll do."

Joey scratches Luna under the halter and behind her ears where the hair is matted down into thick clumps. He lifts the noseband and scratches the bald space where the halter has rubbed the hair away. White flakes of dry, crusty skin flick into the air. Luna is rolling her tongue around in her mouth like a lollipop. She swallows. She yawns. She drops her head some more. Joey reaches for the brass buckle and pulls out the metal pin that locks it in place. He slides the noseband halfway off her face and then raises it again. Buckles it. He looks at me. I nod to go ahead. He releases the buckle again, slides the noseband off Luna's face, and places the halter on the ground. The scar is now visible. Six inches in a zigzag crack that goes from the middle of her nose to the corner of her left eye. Some hair has grown back but it's spotty, scar tissue fills in the blank spaces. Joey rubs her face with the blunt end of his fingertips.

Luna leans in, her head almost touching his chest.

ROOTBEER

April / 2014

"We haven't had her out in a good while," the tall cowboy who meets me at the horse shelter gate tells me. He squashes his flapping cowboy hat to his head, then reaches into the rear pocket of his tight-fitting jeans for a pinch of chewing tobacco. He opens his mouth to press the lump into his already balled-up cheek. I can see his teeth are stained the color of dark coffee. "I'd train her myself if I could, she's my favorite," he murmurs through the wad in his mouth.

"What's her name?" I ask him.

"We call her Rootbeer. I've been trying to get the boss to let me work her." He tucks the tin back into his pocket. "They tell me I'm too tall. But I like 'em short and agile, like her. She'll work out for you. You'll just have to get her mind."

He's half my age, with half my experience, and still he's free to give me advice.

Two weeks earlier my veterinarian had called to ask if I wanted to participate in the first one-hundred-day horse challenge for the Santa Fe Horse Shelter. The shelter is a nonprofit that takes in unwanted horses. Each trainer will train a shelter horse for one hundred days. There will be a competition to choose the winner, and an auction afterward to place the horses into good homes.

I wasn't interested at first. My summer schedule was already filling up, and it was only the middle of March. When I saw her photo on the horse shelter's website, I changed my mind. It could be a good challenge for the residents, I thought. Eliza and Tony would love to have another horse to work. Except for Luna, all the ranch horses are going well under saddle. I printed the photograph and took it over to the ranch. Everyone gathered around to get a closer look.

"She is cute," Tony spoke up first. "I'd love to work with her. Look at those eyes."

In March, Tony, Randy, and I had our one-year anniversary, with Eliza coming in a few months later. Tony is a different man. He greets me with long hugs and fills my ear about how well the horses and residents are doing. His hair, which was a patchwork of haphazard fuzz, has grown in thick and shiny. He parts it to the side now. He has a new set of upper and lower teeth that at first pushed his lips away from his face, making him look like he was ready for a permanent kiss. His lips finally relaxed and rested back against his teeth. Where once there were only gums and a few broken, gray snags of enamel, there are now big, white, friendly incisors.

"You think we can do it?" Randy asked, and before I could say a word, Eliza jumped in.

"Of course, Randy. I mean, look what we've done with Estrella, Hawk, Scout, and Billy this last year."

I KNEW I did not want to do this alone. The thought of us working as a team excited me. If we could do this together, train Rootbeer in one hundred days, we could find her a new home and get her out of the shelter. We could give her a new beginning, a fresh new start.

She came from east of Albuquerque, I was told by the shelter staff, skinny as a rail, alongside her mother and brother. Each of them two to three hundred pounds underweight. They were found in an abandoned corral, no food or water for who knows how long. Her brother didn't make it. He died a few days after their arrival at the shelter.

She is small yet put together like some of the best cutting horses I've seen. Her head, her neck, her back and loin all look of equal length and size. Nothing is out of place. Like the body of a perfectly balanced dancer. Without even watching her take a step, I can already see how beautifully her body will move.

She watches me as I stand on the other side of her water tank. She seems honest and interested, but there's something else, too—something certain, something claimed, something she'll have to let go. When I walk toward her with a lead rope, she lopes off like a deer to the far corner of her corral.

"Here, let me help you, miss." The skinny cowboy walks up behind me with his lariat coiled in his hand.

"No, thanks. I've got it. I'm good." I turn halfway around and give him a big western nod. He stops in his tracks.

Rootbeer bends around to face me as I come near. I stop thirty feet in front of her, feeling like just a few feet closer and she might run. Instead she walks off to her right. Her stride is equal and cadenced. The length and strength of her hindquarters helps her cover a good deal of ground for a small horse. *She'll be great on the trails*, I think to myself. I follow her, walking parallel with her line of travel, lining my body with the middle of her ribcage. She stops, then bends around again, watching me, then turns and walks to the left. I pivot and mimic her movement. We do this back-and-forth thing for a few short minutes before she faces me, pauses, takes four strides toward me, and stands quietly. She seems to think I know what I'm doing.

The competition will be in early July. There are nine very good trainers in the event. Ten total, including us. It doesn't matter if we win. What matters is that we help Rootbeer leave the shelter and get a new home.

I reach over Rootbeer's neck and tie a knot in my rope halter next to her cheek. She follows me out of the corral and down a sandy alley that passes a dozen or more shelter horses. All the horses run to the top of their corrals to watch her pass. She squeals at them. She pins her ears. She lifts one hind leg up in a gesture of *get back*. Already, I know she's the right horse for us.

"She ain't been in no trailer since she came here, miss." The cowboy returns with his lariat. He spits a thin stream of chew from the corner of his lip. "I can put a rope behind her if she needs it," he tells me.

"She's leading pretty good," I point out. "Let's just see how it goes." Rootbeer and I walk past him. I swing the trailer door open. Moo is tied inside, waiting patiently to escort her out of the shelter. Rootbeer jumps right into my trailer. She arches her neck and pins her ears at Moo, who takes one quick sniff of her, then backs away. Her perfectly made, tiny brown body stands quietly, facing the trailer window, watching the other shelter horses rip around their corrals, kicking up dust. I throw the lead line over her back, shut the trailer door, and hustle around to the driver's side.

"Thanks a bunch," I say and wave back to the cowboy who is standing windswept to the east, with his lariat tapping uselessly against his thigh.

WITH HORSES, it is best to do everything right the first time. Otherwise, you spend all your time undoing the unwanted behavior. That first night, I take Rootbeer and Moo home to my barn. Early the next morning, I go to get her from her stall. She moves away and into a corner, turns and faces me, then raises up on her hind legs like a circus elephant doing a trick. She stays up in the air so long, with her front legs tucked in like a grand-prix jumper, that I begin to chuckle, enjoying the show. She comes back down, then rears in the air again, with her ears bright and pointy. I think I see a smile on her face. Every horse has a signature move. They'll do it for fun out in the pasture, or in their corrals when playing with fellow horse mates. Watching Rootbeer in the air, with her belly exposed to the sun, I understand that she wants to play, that she wants me to know something about her. She's not trying to hurt me. *This is the best of me*, she seems to be saying. *And who are you?*

"Okay, lady, I hear you," I say and move off to her side and behind her left hip. I swing my rope in the direction of her haunch, not to hit her, but to encourage her to move out at a walk, instead of raising her front legs clear into the sky. She steps out around the twelve-foot-by-twelve-foot stall where she's been resting all night. My rope swings and swings, calm and lofty, trying to unlock her feet and move her along. She's not happy about my rope swinging, my directions, my leadership. She gives me the ugly face. Her eyes squint and harden, their corners look sharp, like the tips of arrows.

"Don't you worry, little one, I know how special you are," I tell her. I stop swinging my rope, then move to her left side to put on the halter. I groom my hand along the top of her mane and down to her withers. "Special. Special," I sing, and she loosens her ears back to their upright position.

I lead her to the hitching rail and loosely loop the lead rope around the pipe. I'm sure she's never been tied hard to anything. She feels the light tug of the lead and pulls backward, checking to see if she is still free. As I poke through the brush box looking for the softest brush I can find, I look over and see all four of her hooves settle and balance on the ground. She watches me as I search for the right brush. Her head drops to the level of the rail and she lets out a long sigh. *There are at least three sides to this tiny mare: playful, fierce, and lovable*, I think to myself as I slide the soft horsehair brush across her topline.

FOLLOW ME

May / 2014

Tony swings up on Moo and leads Rootbeer along his side, asking her to follow. The lead line dangles from her chin as she stretches out alongside Moo's big swinging trot. *Clip, clop. Clip, clop.* Their legs move along in a diagonal rhythm, cadenced and clear.

There is something about Rootbeer we all love. We know she comes from neglect and starvation. We know she has a strong will to survive. Yet she trusts us. Everything we ask she takes to diligently. She never questions us. She puts her nose to the ground and sniffs, then steps her hooves across the blue plastic tarp without hesitation. She stands with her ears listening backward, as we take the saddle on and off. She humps up her backbone when we cinch her girth, but then walks off without a spook or buck. I wonder how she knows that we are good. That we will be kind.

That we will be generous with her. I wonder how any of us ever know this about one another.

I have started plenty of horses over the years. Most of them, at one time or another, will use their instincts to flee when the pressure gets too great. They will jerk against my rope, race about the round pen, leaping with all four legs above the ground, trying to figure out how to get rid of this thing tied to their back. But not Rootbeer.

When Tony or Eliza swing on and off her back quickly, to get her accustomed to the weight of a human, she twists her nose around and puffs at their knees. She's keeping track. She wants to know who is up there and what they are doing. When Eliza takes the lead rope and bends Rootbeer's neck, her head swings around gently, like ribbon in the wind. She is full of curiosity. When Tony walks her across the ground poles, around the barrels, and through the semitruck tires, wrinkles fold and bevel above her eyes. She measures each footfall with determined concentration. For the first time in my career, I have met a horse who isn't afraid of anything.

Tony wants to be the first on her back. I ask him to wear the big blue riding helmet I brought over for his safety. He's in the round pen, standing on Rootbeer's left side, hopping up and down in the stirrup. She stands quiet and unconcerned. Tony swings up and rests down on her back, then reaches over to put his right foot into the stirrup.

"You can release me," he tells me. "I think she'll be fine."

We both have a rope snapped to her halter. Tony has the lead line, which he'll use to bend and steer her. I have a longer rope, which will act as a tether if Rootbeer gets nervous. This is the first unbroke horse Tony has ever started. I need to be close to him should Rootbeer get excited.

I remind him, "I'm here, Tony, not going anywhere." His neck and head tilt forward with disappointment.

Rootbeer and Tony stand in front of me. Tony smooches a sound from his puckered lips to ask Rootbeer to move forward. He flutters his legs like flags flapping against her ribcage, asking her to move out. Rootbeer looks confused. She holds a wide stance, trying to balance the weight of Tony. Her ears rotate sideways, wondering what he wants her to do.

I step a few strides away and gently toss the end of my rope in the direction of her hindquarters. By now she knows this means "go." Yet still she remains uncertain and refuses to move ahead. Tony keeps making kissing noises and waves his legs out wider. I'm swinging the rope over and under, over and under, when, out of nowhere, Rootbeer begins to slide backward. She loads all her weight onto her hindquarters. Her front legs stiffen and push against her shoulders. We see her forehand rise, as her rear end disappears underneath.

"Whoa! Whoa! Whoa! What is she doing?" Tony shouts. Rootbeer continues to slide backward. She sits down on her haunch, like a dog begging for a biscuit, and Tony slides off her backside. The back pockets of his jeans land first into the sand. His legs splay out of the stirrups and rest on either side of her body. Tony is laughing, and I am, too. Rootbeer remains sitting in the dirt with the saddle still in position. Tony picks himself off the ground. He walks around to Rootbeer's head and starts scratching her behind one ear.

"What are you doing, little girl?" He smiles, then rubs behind the other ear.

It is funny. It's not something I've seen before. Rootbeer couldn't figure out which way to move. She could have bolted, she could have reared. She could have rounded her back and bucked Tony right off. All of these would have been reasonable choices. Instead, she just sat down.

"Come on, sweetie; let's get up." Tony takes the lead rope and gestures for her to stand. She shoves her butt off the ground, then takes a full body shake, sending the leather fenders and stirrups slapping against her sides.

"She'll follow me." Eliza jumps the round-pen rail and takes the long rope from my hand. I let her have it without hesitation. Watching Eliza and Tony working as a team over these past few weeks has been an unexpected pleasure. Something I'm beginning to crave more of in my own life.

"Swing back up," she tells Tony. Rootbeer rests her muzzle against Eliza's forearm and starts nibbling at her long-sleeve T-shirt. Tony gets back in the saddle but hangs onto the horn, just in case of a repeat performance.

Cluck. Cluck. Eliza sucks her tongue off the roof of her mouth and starts walking to her left. Rootbeer ambles along beside her, with Tony chuckling from above.

"FEEL FOR THE MOMENT her hind leg swings underneath," I tell Eliza. She and Tony have been riding Rootbeer for about a month, in and out of the round pen. It's time to teach all three of them the nuance of signals that go into making a nice riding horse. Eliza and Rootbeer ride around me on a circle tracking left.

"I'll call it out," I tell Eliza as she sways along in the saddle. "Your hips swing left, then they swing right. When they swing right, that means her hind leg is coming under. Tap her with your heel. Turn her to the left."

Nothing makes a horse happier than a rider who is thinking

about the footfall of their hooves. It is the most intimate line of communication.

"Now . . . Now . . . Now. Can you feel it?" I ask Eliza.

Eliza has enough focus these days to run this ranch. When I first met her, she couldn't look up, couldn't meet my eye, couldn't speak a sentence. Her growth has come on rapidly. Recently, Daniel and James have moved her into the business office. They want to teach her how to run the accounting system. They challenge her, they pressure her, they support her. Everyone has high hopes for Eliza. She told me a few days back that Daniel would like her off the horse program. He wants her to focus more on the needs of the ranch. She told him she couldn't, that the horses are what keep her grounded.

Eliza told me that when she first arrived, she didn't listen to anyone. People would talk to her, but she couldn't hear a word they said. The only thing she heard was the sound of her own voice bouncing off the inside of her head. Then, early one morning, before first light, she heard the horses muttering from the corrals. She sat up and wondered if someone had forgotten to feed them. That was the first time she thought about anybody besides herself in seven years.

"I feel it," she says, adjusting her posture in the saddle. She taps Rootbeer on the ribs with her left boot heel and turns.

"Timing and cadence," I tell her, "that's what makes a good rider." She turns and walks a circle to the right. She's looking ahead, watching the cottonwood branches blow in the wind at the far end of the pasture. Her head oscillates side to side, moving in rhythm with Rootbeer's feet.

"Now . . . Now . . . Now?" she questions. She's right on the mark. *Tap. Tap.* Her right boot knocks against Rootbeer's side and they turn again.

Tony stands next to me. His mouth is half-open as he pushes his breath in and out, in time with Rootbeer's step. I look to the side and see him with his hands out in front, holding imaginary reins. His body wags along with Eliza's hips.

"Can I try it at the trot?" Eliza asks.

"Yeah!" Tony yells. He can't contain himself.

"Not today," I tell them both. "We have time. Lots of time."

One thing I have learned about recovering addicts—they always want more.

TO THE RIVER

June / 2014

Tony and Eliza meet me at the gate and jump into the back seat of my truck.

"They're not going to let us ride in the competition," Eliza rushes to tell me. "They say we can't do a public event as long as we're still serving our time."

"What?" I'm shocked. "No one can come? No one at all?"

"They haven't said that for certain." I can see Tony in my rearview mirror. He's leaning toward me with his shoulders gathered tightly around his neck. "They said maybe we can go. But only under supervision. And we definitely can't ride."

Tony and Eliza are Rootbeer's people. They are the only ones who have ridden her. I should have been told this sooner. This rule seems to have sprung out of nowhere. Changes like these are common here. The leadership likes to shake things up. They test the residents' patience, their willingness to adapt, their ability to work things out—especially once they get frustrated. I've witnessed this kind of upheaval on the ranch. But this is the first time the test has been pointed at me. I feel my anger start to roil up my back.

"What are we going to do? Will I have to ride her?" I say in a panic, driving toward the corrals and parking under the old cottonwood tree.

"Marcus will!" Tony launches. "He came to brunch on Sunday, and we asked him if he would ride Rootbeer. He said he'd love to ride a horse again."

"Marcus? He hasn't ridden a horse since he's been out." I'm getting a knot in my gut. After all the effort we have put into Rootbeer, now it's either Marcus or myself riding her in the competition? I would have never signed us up if I knew they weren't going to let Tony or Eliza ride. I hate this feeling of not being in control.

I jump down from my truck and walk toward Randy, who is grooming Hawk at the hitching rail. I remember when Randy had to excuse himself regularly to deal with his fits of anger. I turn away from Randy and walk over to Willie's gate and grab a hold, pushing myself back and forth, like Randy used to, trying to keep his temper from flying out of control.

"It's not right. It's not right," I say as I shove myself off the gate.

Randy walks over and pries my fingers from the metal, spreads his arms wide, and gives me a hug. "It'll be alright, Ginger. Rootbeer will be alright." Randy's warm body wraps around me like a soft blanket. I feel my anger dissipate into the well of his chest. Not only can he control his own anger, he can now help me with my own. I feel as small as a pencil inside his wide, thick arms.

Tony and Eliza have put in long hours with Rootbeer, and

they deserve to ride her in the competition. They can walk, trot, and lope her all over this small ranch. She trots through every obstacle, and last week Eliza started jumping her over the two-foot-high crossbeams. This week she's clearing a three-foot jump. I can't imagine doing this without Eliza and Tony.

"It's okay," Eliza comes up behind us. Randy releases me but keeps his arm wrapped around my shoulders. "Rootbeer's gonna have to get off this ranch at some point. I think she's ready. Maybe this is a good thing."

I have known that Rootbeer should get off the ranch. That she will need to travel on open land to see how she adapts. I have wondered how she will do in the mountains. If she'll feel comfortable crossing water. We will need more than these seventeen acres to get her ready. Not just for the competition, but for her potential new owner.

"If we can't ride her," Tony says as he walks up to the three of us, "then at least someone from the livestock team can." Eliza and Tony have already made the adjustment. As usual, I'm the only one clinging to the past.

I have run into Marcus many times down at the gas station in one of the nearby towns. He's working two jobs. At night he works at a restaurant, and during the day he's still working the first job he got when he left the ranch, driving trucks. Being able to hold down a job for a long period of time is one of the success signs of an addict in recovery. Marcus is holding down two jobs. Last time I saw him, he showed me his new used Chevy truck that he bought down in Albuquerque.

"Call Marcus," Tony tells me. "He's waiting for you."

MARCUS AND I follow the arroyo east toward the mountains. I tie a pack behind Rootbeer's saddle. It will carry our lunch, snacks, and enough bottled water to last all day. I pack the rain gear onto Moo's saddle. We'll start east toward Truchas for a few hours, then turn south on an old cattle trail, following the barrancas just north of Chimayó. From there we will head west and downhill toward the Rio Grande. It will take close to five hours to make the loop.

Rootbeer leads the way, and Moo follows. Her steps are long and quick. I ask Moo to trot and catch up. The saddlebags bump against Rootbeer's loins as she marches up the arroyo. Her tail floats side to side, not once noticing the water bottles jostling inside the bags. This is Marcus's fourth ride on her. She made the change from Eliza and Tony without a hiccup. That's a good sign. She'll need to make the change again with her new owner.

After an hour, deep into the desert, we arrive at Ojito, an isolated farm surrounded by wide open BLM land. Ojito is owned by a friend of mine. Way out here, in the middle of the desert, Ojito sits on spring-fed land. Cottonwood, russian olive, and elm trees rise above the piñon and juniper drylands. We walk toward the grove, looking for water and a cool place to rest. Rootbeer wades through the shallow spring that turns into a westward flowing creek. Marcus gives her the reins, and she stretches down to sip and suck the cold, clear water. She's barely sweating. Today there are three clouds in the sky. It's going to get hot. She leaves the creek and heads for the shade of a cottonwood, waiting for Moo to finish his drink.

We cross the creek and head up the driveway onto the farm. It's mid-June, and the flowers and vegetable gardens are beginning to peak. My friend Sam comes out from his adobe home, looking surprised but happy to have company. I don't see him much, maybe once or twice a year, but when I do it's always on horseback. He is a bit of a hermit, living out here. His face shows three-week stubble, almost a beard. He's barefoot. When he looks up at me, he gives a wide grin. I can see something green stuck to his upper teeth. I wonder if Sam owns a mirror.

"Hey, Sam, this is Marcus and Rootbeer, new friends of mine." Sam walks over and shakes Marcus's hand. Marcus looks around the property. The carcasses of rusted-out cars lie in a tangle of weeds. Two ancient homesteads are melting back into the earth. An old cat is licking rainwater from a broken toilet thrown into Sam's front yard.

"How long have you lived out here?" Marcus asks Sam.

"You want some zucchinis?" Sam asks, looking up at Marcus, ignoring the question. "They just started coming in." Sam doesn't get many visitors out here. I don't know how often he goes to town.

"Sure," I say to Sam.

Marcus is tongue-tied.

Sam starts scratching Rootbeer's chest. "Now this is the kind of horse I need around here. Don't you think?" Sam's still staring up at Marcus.

"Yes, sir, that's right," Marcus says with a newfound confidence. "A horse like Rootbeer can take you anywhere you need to go out here."

Sam leads us on a path that winds through his vegetable gardens. The raised beds are full of horse manure, which Sam comes and gets from me in the fall. The spinach and lettuce leaves are just about to bolt. His squash, zucchini, peppers, and tomatoes have healthy dark-green leaves with flowers ripening underneath. Rootbeer walks through the garden slowly, looking at every little thing. She's at home in this world of natural wonder, occasionally stretching her neck down to smell the plants. The trail takes us back to Sam's house.

"We're heading to Chimayo, then back to the river," I tell Sam. "I'm glad you were home; it's so good to see you."

"Wait. Wait just a minute." Sam runs inside and comes out with a beautiful tie-dyed bandana wrapped around four perfectly grown zucchinis. He unzips the flap on my saddle bag and lays them across our raincoats.

"Thank you, dear Sam." I reach over Moo's neck and give Sam a big hug. He smells like he hasn't showered in days. "Just knowing you are here, under this great big sky, growing food, and living just how you want to, always makes me feel better."

"You be safe," he tells me and holds onto my hand a little longer. There are only a few men—I can count them all on one hand—who make me feel equal. Sam is one of them.

We rein the horses around, and head back into the arroyo, heading east.

For the next hour we trot and lope, climbing increasingly taller hills until we hit the edge of the national forest. Small pines and large junipers mark the change in elevation. Rootbeer switches her lead at every curve in the arroyo. She flattens her neck and catches the rhythm of a rocking-chair canter. Marcus barely moves on top of her.

Up ahead I see the bloated body of a dead animal. The stench is thick and fresh, three days old at the most. A committee of vultures views us coming and land atop a large pine.

"Let's track to the right of that," I try to tell Marcus, but he's too far ahead and doesn't hear me. He heads straight for it. Moo shies to the right, side passing around thickets of cholla, trying to avoid the swelling stink. We catch up to Rootbeer on the other side.

"Looked like an old dog," Marcus tells me as I run up behind him and Rootbeer. "Someone must have driven it all the way out here to put him out of his misery." *Food for the wildlife.* Many locals think this way. "Rootbeer took one look at it and kept going." Marcus is proud of her.

Back at a trot, we follow another curve of the arroyo. The landscape is getting rocky and is studded with small trees.

Midday we turn right onto the cattle trail, heading south. We pass a group of dirt bikers, the only other people we see all day. Their bikes are screaming through the hills around us. The high-pitched squeal of their engines startles Moo. He jumps forward, then sideways. The whirling engines echo off every hill. Moo takes off ahead of Rootbeer, snorting three times, letting her know there's trouble all around.

When Moo gets like this, I know not to hold him back. I try to keep him on the trail, but he runs up a short hill, then stands at the top searching for Rootbeer. She and Marcus are walking below us on the trail, dirt bikers swirling on the hills above them. Moo lets out a scream when he sees her. *Over here*, he tells her. She looks up and mutters softly, letting Moo know she's coming along.

"She's fantastic," I tell Marcus when we meet up again. He has spent most of this day rubbing the mane on Rootbeer's topline, back and forth.

She can climb anything. Marcus takes her up one of the last barrancas, before we turn west, downhill to the river. She scales the sharp incline with her head low, her hindquarters digging and pushing up the sandy slope. The ridge is short and thin, her hooves send sand and rock tumbling off the edge. Her haunches look like a pair of skis tucked deep under her torso, as she readies herself to descend.

"Tough but kind." That's what Tony said about her when I asked him to give me his opinion. Eliza said she was "smart and determined." I said, "loving and independent." It's curious how we see everything from the same small perspective from which we see ourselves.

MOO WADES INTO the four-foot-high water of the Rio Grande and takes a long drink. The water reaches his belly. Rootbeer looks concerned about dropping down the bank. It's covered in tall grass and black, sinking mud. Marcus gives her time. He sets his reins down, right in front of the saddle horn. She snakes her neck left and right, looking for the correct route to get to the river.

Rootbeer sniffs and snorts. She has her one brief moment of panic, weaving back and forth along the bank. Stepping forward, then rushing backward when the bank collapses under her hooves. Marcus just sits there, waiting for her to figure things out. In less than a minute, Rootbeer is belly deep in the river, with her nose plunged below the surface.

JUST A FEW

July / 2014

The rain came down hard last night, an inch and a half in two hours. With the morning heat the humidity began to rise. It's seven a.m. and the sweat drips down our backs as Marcus and I load the obstacle course into my trailer. The competition starts today at noon.

Each trainer will have ten minutes to show their horse in front of the judge and the crowd. Tony and Eliza have designed and built the course for Marcus and Rootbeer to ride through. We've been practicing the pattern for the last three weeks. Rootbeer runs through the course with ease as Marcus barely steers her, the reins dangling from her neck. Marcus sits in the saddle as if he were sitting in a comfy chair.

Rootbeer likes Marcus. She calls to him in a soft mutter when he drives onto the ranch in his older Chevy pickup. She mutters when he grooms her, when he saddles her, when he mounts her. She mutters again when he gets off. He's just the right size for Rootbeer. They make a good-looking pair.

Marcus drags two poles into my trailer. I follow behind dragging one. We need to stack all the obstacles in the front, to leave room for Rootbeer to load in the back. We arrange the poles in a tight bundle as moisture drips off our cheeks. Marcus smells like cologne and cigarettes. He's been dating lately, and maybe last night he was out late. His perspiration smells like meat and sex.

We finish loading and make plans to meet at the showgrounds by 10:30. We will have an hour to warm Rootbeer up before the competition.

Eliza and Olivia have been cleared to leave the ranch and attend the competition. A guy named Charlie, whom I've only spoken to a few times, will be their driver and supervisor. Charlie's been on the ranch for more than five years. He's long been finished with his parole and prison term. He stays at the ranch to continue to mentor the younger men. Charlie is bald, plump, and very pale. I told him to make sure to bring a hat, some sunscreen, and something to keep him cool on this long, hot day. It is projected to rise over one hundred degrees.

Tony and Randy were not approved to come off the ranch. I don't know how or why these decisions were made. All I know is, Tony is heartbroken. He had tears in his eyes when he told me the news. I promised him that we would make sure to videotape Rootbeer's ride. That didn't cheer him up. *It doesn't feel fair*, I thought to myself, as I wrapped my arms around Tony's defeated body. I'll have to trust Daniel and James's reasoning.

There are many things that happen at this ranch that I know
nothing about.

DRIVING ONTO THE SHOWGROUNDS, I see that the large outdoor
arena to my right is completely flooded from last night's rain. It's
a five-hundred-foot oval, and the middle of it looks like a swim-
ming pool. Both ends are dry and there is a dry path around the
perimeter, but the middle has at least four inches of standing water.

I recognize the two trainers working their horses around the
giant puddle. Donna is from Albuquerque, a western trainer just
learning about dressage. She's working a small gray gelding who
looks at least part mustang. He has a short neck and back, big
bony legs, with a long flowing mane and tail. Donna's working
him from the ground at the edge of the makeshift pond. She's
trying to settle him down, but he's not sure about all this water.

Laurie and Pete are at the other dry end of the arena with
a long-legged chestnut mare who looks two hands taller than
Rootbeer. I've known Laurie for years. I gave her lessons on her
Missouri Fox Trotter when he was young and very excitable. The
mare they have for this competition is visibly talented. She trots
around Pete with her knees and hocks bouncing off the ground;
her back barely moves. *I bet she's a smooth ride*, I think to myself.

It is good to see my fellow trainers, my friends, with their
horses from the shelter. I have been looking forward to seeing
how their horses are doing. We have all been working hard to
make this day successful.

I look up and see Eliza waving me over. She, Olivia, and
Charlie have set up a tented booth with a hanging banner across
the front announcing the DS Ranch. They have tables filled with
brochures about the mission of the ranch. They brought a big,

white cooler full of water and juice, and enough chairs to have a small party. Olivia and Eliza are beaming with excitement.

I park near an empty corral, and we unload Rootbeer. She gets off the trailer slowly, then looks around the fairgrounds like she's been here a thousand times. Eliza and Olivia want to take her for a walk to show her around. They look beautiful. Their hair is down and unrestrained, and it drapes across their shoulders. They are both dressed in stylish western blouses with brand-new, donated Wrangler jeans. I have never seen them in makeup before. Today there's blush, eye shadow, and lipstick. Just looking at them, together with Rootbeer, makes me feel like we've already won.

Charlie helps me unload the obstacles. The event organizers come by our booth and ask to see Rootbeer. Olivia and Eliza have walked her into a swarm of adoring people over by the food trucks. Everyone is trying to touch her.

"She's over there," I point her out for the organizers. "It looks like she already has some fans."

I wave to Eliza to bring Rootbeer back. We need to brush her down, comb and braid her mane, and wipe her body down with Showsheen, a liquid product that will make her coat look shiny. The organizers said that they are expecting over three hundred people today. The cars and trucks keep rolling in. I look at my phone and see it's already eleven. Marcus is late. The announcer makes a call across the loudspeaker.

"Trainers, the arena is open. You have forty minutes to warm up your horses."

We finish dolling up Rootbeer, and Eliza gets her saddled. Olivia goes to the trailer and brings me the bridle. I'll have to warm her up until Marcus arrives. I go to the tack room for my boots and hat, then mount Rootbeer, and head to the arena.

We turn right past the gate and walk the rail heading toward the covered grandstand. Huge speakers blare country music into our faces. The stands are filling quickly. There are umbrellas, rowdy children, and older women wearing floppy hats. A large man carries two identical chihuahuas on his shoulders. There's a guy hanging an oversized American flag along the front of the grandstand. He looks like a monkey hanging off the rail. Rootbeer walks by all of it. She turns and faces the crowd. Her ears flip sideways: tall, pointy, and curious. Three little girls come running down the aisle, reaching through the fence barrier, trying to pet Rootbeer's nose. I ask her to step up toward the little waving hands. She moves into their touch without hesitation.

The other trainers are trotting by behind us. I turn in the saddle to watch them go. Maybe it's this special day. Maybe it's the crowd coming in. Maybe it's me being romantic. But every one of these horses takes my breath away. I feel so grateful to be on top of Rootbeer, just for these few moments, before Marcus arrives. I click Rootbeer into a trot, then up to a lope, and we roll away from the grandstand heading left. We cut across the middle of the pond, splashing through the water in a three-beat rhythm. *Ta ta spash. Ta ta splash. Ta ta splash.* Rootbeer never looks down at the water. We head over to the far wall, where the bright, waving sponsorship banners are hanging. The breeze picks them up and lays them back down. Rootbeer walks beside them unconcerned.

I look back toward the gate for Marcus and see Eliza heading into the muddy arena with her nice clean jeans dragging on the ground. Rootbeer and I hustle over to meet her.

"Marcus is here," she tells me. "I think, I mean I don't know, but I think he's drunk. He's wearing this bad cologne. Olivia said she smelled alcohol." I remember the cologne, the cigarettes, the sex smell from this morning.

"Where is he?" I ask.

"He's in the bathroom. He'll be right out."

I wait for Marcus by the gate. People I don't know are coming over to tell me how cute Rootbeer looks. I stare straight at them but can barely speak. If he's drunk, what will I do? What if I can't smell it? Should I ask him flat out if he's been drinking? He'll probably deny it. A young woman walks over and puts her hand on my knee to get my attention. She's looking for a new horse and asks me how old is Rootbeer. I feel the touch of her gentle hand on my knee. *She would be perfect for Rootbeer.* This hopeful thought relieves me from my sinking desperation.

Marcus walks over and stands beneath me. His eyes are clear, and he's smiling. He's dressed nicely, in black jeans with a neatly pressed white button-down shirt. He's wearing the free cowboy boots the ranch gave him before he left on his work out. There's a gold chain around his neck, and his curly hair is neatly combed and off to one side. I can't smell anything except his cologne. He looks totally sober.

"Sorry I'm late," he says. "I got stuck in traffic in Pojoaque. There was a bad accident." He turns and addresses the young woman next to me. "She's a great horse," he tells her. "I've been riding her for about a month. It has been so fun." He reaches over to Rootbeer, scratches her behind her ears, and she mutters to him.

I decide to let him mount and take Rootbeer around the arena. I still can't smell the alcohol. He isn't acting any different than he has over this last month. He walks along the rail, staying out of the mud and the swimming-pool areas. He takes Rootbeer around the perimeter of the oval, walking past the other trainers and introducing himself.

Eliza and Olivia are standing by my side as we watch them walk along.

"I couldn't smell any alcohol," I tell them. "I don't know what else to do."

Marcus and Rootbeer walk past the banners on the far side and start into a trot. I'm watching every movement of his hands and legs, looking for something that seems out of character. They round the far wall of the arena and head along the rail toward the grandstand. As they approach the grandstand, Rootbeer comes to a dead halt. Marcus taps her with the heel of his boot. She won't go. He taps her again, and again. Rootbeer takes her right hind leg and swings it far under her belly and knocks Marcus's right boot out of the stirrup. Marcus looks back at Rootbeer's hind leg in surprise. He looks up, searching for me in the crowd of people. He doesn't know what to do. He can't get her to take another step. He bends her neck around and tries to face her the other direction. She won't budge.

I run through the gate along the rail and past the grandstand, now crammed with hundreds of spectators. I stop next to Rootbeer's shoulder and lean in close. Marcus is right above me. The sun is high, it must be ninety-five degrees. The armpits of his clean white shirt are soaked. The cologne has worn off. I smell alcohol seeping from his body.

"You've been drinking," I tell him.

"Just a few, nothing much," he shrugs off my accusation.

I know Marcus's father is an alcoholic. He has told me this over these last few weeks.

"He's a functional alcoholic," Marcus told me. His father has held a retail job for twenty years. Last year his boss put him on leave and encouraged him to get some help. Marcus said his father has cut back on the Jim Beam, but he still drinks a six-pack a night, along with a bottle of wine. He said his father is back to work and doing just fine.

"Drinking's never been my problem," Marcus told me on the trail two days ago. "Heroin is what got me messed up."

I realize now that Marcus believes he can be a functional drunk, just like his dad. He thinks he can drink as much as he wants and still hold down a job, still be able to ride a horse. Rootbeer thinks otherwise.

"A few is a few too many for me, Marcus." I ask him to dismount. "You're either totally clean or I can't help you. I can't let you ride." I'm not angry. I look right into Marcus's eyes, still trying to reach out so he can see I'm not turning my back on him. "You took a wrong turn, man. I hope you can see that. You know how to get back; you can figure this out. I know you can. But you need to get some help." My voice is low, I speak so no one around us can hear. I want to show him the respect he's earned, but I must tell him the truth.

The three of us walk toward the gate together, Marcus and I staring at the ground. I wonder what Rootbeer knows and how she knows it. She felt the cloudy, self-destructive edge of our humanity and refused to participate. I wish I was more like Rootbeer, I wish I could be that clear. Maybe, if I keep doing the work I'm doing, maybe one day, I'll get close. I watch Marcus turn left away from me, walking out of the arena with his neck and shoulders rolled forward and over his chest. I haven't seen this round, defeated shape of a body in many months. I pinch away the tears forming in the corner of my eyes.

The announcer's voice squeals out of the loudspeaker. "Riders, you have five more minutes."

WAVES

July / 2014

I walk Rootbeer back to my trailer where a crowd of my horse clients have gathered. They have heard me talk about Rootbeer for months and now, finally, they get to meet her. Becky, a client from Austin, Texas, takes the lead rope from my hand and starts grooming the dust off Rootbeer's coat. Janet and Sue are gushing over how cute she is. Francine, who owns a huge warmblood, keeps saying how much she's always wanted a small horse. Glenda, my partner, has also arrived. She can see in my face that something's wrong.

"I'm going to ride her," I tell her. "Marcus has been drinking." She takes a big sigh. She knows how disappointed I must be.

There is no time to wallow. I have five minutes to clean myself up, brush my hair, and get the obstacles ready. Eliza, Olivia, and Charlie rush over.

"Where's Marcus?" Eliza asks. I point toward the food truck, where Marcus is talking on his cell phone. He is still folded forward in a slump. I hope he stays for Rootbeer's ride. I hope that somehow this day will help him figure things out.

"Can anyone drive a stick shift?" I ask the three of them. We need to load the obstacles into the bed of my truck. We will drive them into the arena when it's Rootbeer's turn to go. They have allowed us only five minutes to prepare the arena for our demonstration.

"I can drive the truck," Charlie tells me. We load all the obstacles into the back of my truck, and Charlie drives it to the arena and parks it near the gate. Eliza and Olivia know the pattern by heart, they can set up the obstacles, one at a time, while Charlie puts the truck in four-wheel drive and makes his way around the ring.

Becky walks Rootbeer over and meets us at the gate. All the competition horses and their trainers are standing nearby. We draw straws. Rootbeer and I will go third. That gives me a little time. I go to the back of my truck and pull the bright, multicolored parachute out of its bag. The wind has picked up and blows the crackling sheet of fabric into a giant bubble. All the horses start to spook. All except Rootbeer. I get the rope from the bag, attach it to the parachute, and hand it to Eliza.

"Meet me over by the back of the grandstand," I tell her, swinging up on Rootbeer. Rootbeer and I practice dragging the parachute behind the bleachers at a walk. I'll enter the arena at a lope, dragging this puffy, billowing bunch of fabric behind me. Rootbeer has been dragging it for weeks now and couldn't care less. I wrap the rope around the horn and trail the parachute off her right hip.

"Ginger!" I hear someone call my name from up above.

It is Carla and John, clients of mine who live in El Dorado.

Carla told me last week during our lesson that they would be at the event. They are looking for a new horse for John. I told them about Rootbeer. How I thought she would be a great horse for the trail. John is older, and he needs something low to the ground and steady.

"Is that Rootbeer?" Carla screams over the noise of the crowd.

I wave to her. Rootbeer keeps trucking along, dragging what looks like a deflated monster behind her. John and the two guys sitting next to him turn around in their seats and stare down at us.

I'm thinking about the pattern. When to drop the parachute, and where I start the obstacle course. I lay my calf softly against Rootbeer's side. She bends and turns right. I lay my other leg against her. She bends and turns left. In one hundred days, Tony and Eliza have brought Rootbeer further than any colt I've ever started.

Eliza walks over. "You better get to the gate, you're next."

I've always felt riding a horse was like riding a wave. The wave rolls you along. You don't kick the wave, or beat it, or even think you can control it. Every wave is unique. Some gather height quickly and close out fast. Some come in thin and build slowly. They make a smooth tunnel, no wake on their surface. You see the wave coming. You angle your board. You prepare your body to paddle. But once the wave turns over its lip and has you in its grasp, all you can do is glide along the surface like a lover.

Many horses have taught me this, but Spirit, a little gray Arab, was the one I'll always remember. She wasn't mine to train. The owner had chosen to put her in training with another trainer at one of the barns where I ride. I could tell the trainer didn't like her. He tried all his techniques, but still she pinned her ears and spun her tail in circles during every ride he put on her. Eventually he just left her standing all day in a stall.

I don't usually offer to ride horses for free, but when her owners came to pick her up, that's exactly what I did.

"Can you leave her another few months?" I asked them as they prepared to load her back in their trailer. "I wouldn't charge you anything. I'd just like the opportunity to ride her."

They left her with me for three months. I took her for long walks around the ranch. I let her lead out ahead of me, fifteen feet. She was the leader; I was the follower. When I saddled her I never tied her, because I knew she couldn't handle being constrained. On our first ride, I sat on her back for an hour, not asking for anything. We never moved. I got off. The next ride was the same. A week went by. On our seventh ride, she took me for a walk around the outdoor arena. Turning and bending, wherever she wanted to go was fine with me. She'd stop by the gate and watch the other horses being worked in the round pen. We stood there for as long as she wanted, until she was ready to move forward again. It took a great deal of effort to make no effort at all. I lost track of time. I lost track of myself. No longer the trainer, the one who calls all the shots, I wasn't sure what I was.

Spirit loved it. Her ears and eyes flickered lightly as she moved around on her own free will. Her tail swung free and loose, in cadence with her hind legs. We spent weeks riding in the pastures down by the river. Spirit would look up and see the yearlings romping in the field next to us. She'd roll into a trot and head toward the fence line, her head high, watching the youngsters run. I rocked in the saddle along with her. Never telling her where to go. Never telling her how fast or how slow. Never having an opinion at all. I let go of every idea I had about what I wanted, what I should do, what I thought I knew.

"Be an open vessel," one of my teachers always told me. "The more you open, the more they come through." He was talking about riding horses. I was thinking about riding waves.

"AND NEXT UP we have the DS Ranch, riding Rootbeer!" the announcer shouts through the loudspeaker.

Rootbeer and I ride through the gate with the parachute dragging behind us.

We are alone, all by ourselves in this giant oval, and she's waiting for me to start the show. We stand in front of the grandstand, and I bow to the crowd. The clapping of a few hundred people startles her. I lay my hand on her neck.

"It's all about you," I remind her as a breeze comes up. I see the parachute lift off the ground and rise above us. Rootbeer leads off at a lope. The parachute is ten feet in the air and following close behind. *We didn't prepare for this*, I think to myself, but I let her go. We circle left, loping into the water. I see the colorful balloon traveling just off to the side in my periphery. In the three weeks we have been practicing this drill, the parachute has never lifted this high.

We cross the arena, heading for the low jump Eliza has set up in front of the sponsorship banners. Rootbeer lengthens and lowers her neck in preparation. I loosen the reins. Just before the cross rail, she hustles her hind legs underneath and lifts her front legs two feet higher than necessary. At the top of the arch I see the parachute hovering above us. *This*, I think to myself, *this is not something I would have ever thought I'd do, not in a million years.*

We trot a few strides, then lope off to the right. The parachute that is following us seems to be growing. Everyone is clapping. At the far end of the arena I slow down to a trot, and the balloon loses its sail. We halt, and I let the rope that connects us to the parachute drop to the ground.

Rootbeer is calm. I feel my legs wave out, then in, as she takes deep breaths. I'm not sure she even noticed the hovering canopy that made me look like I was parasailing on horseback. Next, we head toward the ground poles. They are spread apart, wide enough so we can hit one stride of canter between each pole. Ever since I first saw her on the shelter's website, I knew her body could do amazing things. She bounces across the ground poles like an elk over a fence.

Past the poles we transition to a trot and weave through the standing boxes of flowers Eliza and Olivia have placed in a long row. Rootbeer's ribs are twisting under my seat. I feel the snake of her spine as she curves between the beautiful flowers, her braided mane swishing against her neck. The weave of her body makes me feel weightless. Like I am no longer made of muscle and bone.

At the end of the flowers, we trot through a narrow channel made of PVC pipes. The two-foot-wide channel takes a sharp right turn and we come to a dead halt. In front of us is a large bell hanging from a post. I reach in front of Rootbeer's muzzle and clang the bell three times. The crowd erupts. We back out of the L-shaped channel, turn left, and take off at a gallop. Splashing through the pond like we are on a movie set, heading straight for the grandstand, full tilt.

I sit back in the saddle and Rootbeer comes to a screeching halt. The crowd in front of us gives a loud applause. Rootbeer looks up and takes in the sight of it. Her head is higher than it has been all day. Underneath the sound of the crowd, I feel the rumble of her soft mutter crawl across her back. My body shimmies with the feel of it.

"THE HORSES HAVE SAVED ME," I hear Eliza tell a woman in a turquoise summer dress who is wearing an expensive Santa Fe cow-girl hat docked on the very top of her head. "I don't know what I would have done if it hadn't been for the horses. They woke me up." Eliza is standing inside the tent, behind the table, meeting this woman's gaze directly in the eye. She smiles and hands the woman a brochure. "This is what we do," she tells her. "We save lives."

OUR TENT IS FILLED with many people I don't know. Everyone is crowded around trying to talk with Eliza, Olivia, or Charlie.

Olivia is talking with my clients Carla and John. They have pulled their chairs under the tent and are engaged in an intense conversation.

"When did you know?" I hear Carla ask Olivia in an inquisitive voice.

Olivia takes her time. She measures her words. "I think I was eight years old," she says. "That's when I realized she was an addict. That she was using when she gave birth to me."

Rootbeer is resting in a nearby corral. She has a pile of hay in front of her. Her eyes are shut as she chews, systematically, on the wad inside her mouth. A third-place ribbon is pinned to the gate. I'm sitting on the fender of my trailer. Glenda gives me a kiss and long hug, then joins me, leaning against the aluminum trailer wall. We watch a crowd of people leave the grandstand and head into our tent. The visitors bend over to read the brochures. They stand up and stare at the three faces in front of them, confused. *Are these three people addicts? Have they been to prison?* What they see, versus what they believe, isn't matching up.

Eliza lifts her voice above the gathering crowd. "Please, come up and take our brochures. I'm sure everyone here has a friend or a loved one who's been in the same position we once were."

Glenda and I sip on a cold bottle of water as we listen to Eliza,

Olivia, and Charlie tell their stories. I've heard most of them before, but Glenda hasn't. We watch the faces of the visitors as they read the brochures.

"It's a ranch," one woman tells her husband. "They trained the horse at their prison-alternative ranch."

John and Carla leave the tent and walk over.

"Ginger, I have one question for you," John asks me. Carla stands by his side, knocking him in the ribs to get the question out. "Do you think I'm too big for her?" He's talking about Rootbeer. Our little Rootbeer. He's going to bid on her in the auction, Carla tells us.

Glenda and I turn to look at Rootbeer. Three girls are hand-feeding her carrots through the corral panels. I think about the first morning I went to get her from my barn. How she reared into the air, looking like a giant Thoroughbred. I remember how Tony slid off her backside on her first ride, as she sat down on her haunches like a dog. How Eliza rode her over three-foot jumps just the other day.

"As a matter of fact, Rootbeer needs a big person," I tell Carla and John. "She's small in body, but not in her mind."

BELLE

North Carolina / 1995

When I raised my hand toward Belle's mouth, she jerked and swung her big bone of a head so fast I fell backward, trying to avoid contact. Her lips pinched shut. Her fine chin hairs poked straight out like porcupine quills trying to fend off my touch. One long muscle, the one that connects her head to her neck to her shoulder, snapped back and forth like a bullwhip. *Forget it*, I told myself. Forget about touching her mouth, her lips, her tongue. I told her, *you keep them*. I don't want them. I don't need them. They were hers and never again to be taken.

Bob had made me a bitless bridle from the thick leather harness he used to drive his team. Back when he drove a pair of Belgian horses around his farm, tilling the fields, every spring and fall.

"She don't need nothin' in her mouth," Bob kept telling me,

hollering in his usual hard-of-hearing, louder-than-necessary voice.

He had sewn a piece of soft leather across the noseband, with fleece tacked onto the underside. One ring sewn on each corner of the nose piece, where he snapped a pair of leather reins.

I moved far away from Belle's mouth and started cleaning her hooves, picking out the stones, the mud, the rolled oats stuck in the grooves next to her frog, leftovers from this morning's breakfast. I picked her hooves up and laid them in the basket of space I built for them between my bent thighs. It was a place of rest, if she could trust it. The top of her hoof touched down on my thigh, then pulled up three times before she accepted my help. It reminded me of dipping my fingers in holy water at the back of church every Sunday when I was a child. It was my favorite part of Mass. Walking into the silence of the church, I would slow my pace and let my family hurry ahead to get the same pew they sat in each week. I came to the holy water like a priest or nun, head bowed with my hands prepared in prayer position. I would face the bowl, go down on one knee, then dip my right hand in the water three times. Not for the Trinity. Not for any reason really. Three was a perfect number. One is lonely. Two is not enough. Three holds magic.

Belle's hoof rested ever so lightly on my jeans. The bottom of it looking right at me, like a face concentrating so hard it distorts itself. The horn wall had separated from the sole and tiny pebbles were stuck in its crack. I took the thin tip of the hoof pick and started plucking them free. Underneath, a thick black goo of summer thrush began to stink in the air. I scraped it out and wiped it on the ground. Flies buzzed around us immediately.

I cleaned one hoof, put it back on the ground slowly, then

checked back on her. As the hoof reset on the earth, she rolled out her thick wet tongue, like a snail poking out from its shell. She touched the tip of it to her dripping nostrils, licked a few times, then curled it back inside the contours of her mouth. After cleaning each hoof, after placing it back on the ground, she repeated the same ritual: parting her lips, coiling her tongue out flat, then licking the salty drips from her flaring nostrils. This is how she began to teach me her language. That her hooves, her mouth, her brain were all connected down and over the long, lovely line of her body. Her legs were sentences that ended at each hoof. Her body needed the touch of the earth to be heard. I began to see every movement she made as a long paragraph, a story, a way to understand each other. I learned to listen with my eyes.

After the last hoof was cleaned, she stood still with her lead line resting on the ground. I still couldn't tie her to anything. Not a tree. Not the barn. Not anything besides my open hand or the soft drape of the rope on the dirt. When tied, Belle would thrash and pull backward in a panic, breaking halters and snapping the hitching post in two. But when she was free, she was as motionless as a great horned owl. Only her eyelids blinked open and shut. I could leave her to get the saddle, to get the brushes, the fly spray, even a drink of water from the hydrant. She wouldn't take a step. Freedom gave her a kind of stillness I craved. When I would return to her, she would lower her muzzle and smell whatever offering I came back with: the saddle pad, the mane and tail conditioner, alfalfa pellets that I would serve to her with my wide open palm. She would tuck her chin close to her chest where her nostrils could meet the new gifts first, then her lips brushed over them, nibbling with the slightest motion that tickled my hand.

Everything was language. Everything had life. She witnessed her world like a monk on a solitary pilgrimage. Sunlight bouncing inside the water trough, bluebirds with their toes wrapped around the top fence wire, calls of faraway dogs, a car door closing at the neighbors'; each event was profoundly important, worthy of recognition. I hadn't seen the world from this vantage point in a very long time.

When I was in first and second grade, I waited for the Catholic school bus at the corner of Elm and New Road. I would get to the bus stop early and sit alone on the white picket fence of my neighbors, listening to the absence of sound. There was barely traffic at that time in the morning, no kids on bicycles, no mothers yelling from inside our neighbors' houses. Sitting atop the fence, I would try to keep my legs from swinging and steady my rump on the top rail. Then I would close my eyes. For just a few minutes, there was absolutely nothing. Silence was the color of white under my eyelids and the smell of morning air before anyone woke and touched it.

Once the bus arrived, I'd sit near the front alone and hold that silence until the clatter from the kids in the back broke it into pieces. Sometimes I recognized it in everyday things: a single fish in a small round bowl, a baby resting in her crib, my grandmother kneeling in prayer in the front pew of the church. I wanted to know nothingness, that place where silence had a language. It seemed to me that other animals knew it. The shorebirds floating past the ocean break. Starfish being washed back and forth inside the rock jetty. Turtles spending all day inside their shell. I knew nothing was something, but I didn't know what. I spent my whole life looking for it, and then I met Belle.

Bob always liked to help me saddle. He was the one Belle trusted to put on her new leather bridle. He would send us off with Bud, his farm dog, leading us down the trail. With only the soft leather strap above her nose, I could steer Belle, pointing her head in the direction of Bud's tail. I barely touched the reins, and rarely did I hold them in my grip. They dangled and swayed alongside her neck as we went into the woods, crossed the creek, and followed the trail that would lead us to the wild-flowers. It was a short climb up a rocky hill, then back down. Belle lowered her head on the downhill, watching for the rise and fall of red-ant hills or a tangle of kudzu crawling across our path. In the woods, she was never afraid. Surefooted, she never spooked or balked or tried to turn for home. With Belle I never tried to be the leader, the number one, the alpha mare. It was always an agreement of our bodies working together. She set that rule, and I followed.

We searched the wet woods for May apple, false Solomon's seal, wintergreen, and black-eyed Susans. I'd climb off Belle's back and walk us into a patch of wild geraniums just to kick their scent into the air. Bud would lie and wait on a nearby hill, resting his head on his forelegs, keeping his eye on us. The low-rolling hills were thick with young trees and grasses. Belle would pick at the grass with her three-year-old incisors, then slide her jaw side to side, chewing the blades into a green mash that spilled from her lips. Her eyes closed as if she was in a dream. We walked through the geraniums, me on foot, looking for a fallen tree trunk to stand on and climb back into the saddle. Tall stalks of black cohosh grew where the trees parted and let sunrays filter down in strips. Riding past them, I could feel their healing medi-cine speak to us.

After touching the holy water with the tips of my fingers, I would walk up the main aisle of the church, past my parents and sisters, toward the oversized, tortured, crucified Jesus hanging on the wall. I bowed my head again, genuflected, and sat down next to my grandmother, who regularly sat alone in the first pew. She would look up from her kneeling, praying position and scooch down the aisle, giving my small body space to enter. Kneeling next to my grandmother, I felt God more than I did anyplace else. Sometimes I thought I could smell God on her breath. Her hairspray was thick and metallic-scented, and it stuck her thin, almost nonexistent hair flat onto her head. As she made the sign of a miniature cross onto her forehead, she would open her mouth and push out a breath—a bouquet of meat and vegetables; turnips, cabbage, pork. The fleshy scent of corporeal earth mingled with the residual aerosol. The mixture smelled like gilded earth, and I knew God wasn't far away. We kneeled there together, young and old knees aching, until the altar boy came out from behind a curtain, and the clink of incense at the end of a long chain raised us to our feet.

BUD, BELLE, AND I passed trillium and hooded columbine on our way uphill to the old oak that stood alone on the highest point of ground in the woods. Its trunk was ten feet around in diameter. All three of us climbed onto the small, flat patch that surrounded the oak. This was our turnaround point. Our listening place. We rested there and stared into the woods that appeared to stretch into forever. A nuthatch hung upside down from the branch above our heads, pecking at the ants climbing in the crevices of bark. From the top of this hill we could see south to the open pastureland where purple martins swayed back and forth over the tall oat grass, picking mosquitoes out of the air. Farm dogs called from the north, past the creek and back toward home. Bud's floppy Labrador ears lifted off his head. Belle let out a big yawn, then curled her upper lip back away from her gums, tilting her muzzle to the sky. There were so many things we loved about these woods. We wanted everything. And nothing at all.

SOFT CREATURES

September / 2014

"Sit. Sit." Tony drags Randy's mounting box close to the round-pen rail and places me down carefully. I've been gone for over six weeks. I've been sick—very sick. My appendix burst while on a four-day horse-packing trip into the mountains near Creede, Colorado. The first day I felt a little queasy. The second day I took three ibuprofen, drank a few beers, and felt better. The third day I couldn't eat and had to take six hundred milligrams of ibuprofen every six hours just to stay upright. The fourth day I headed home. Glenda took me to the emergency room right away.

"You are lucky to be alive," the doctor said to me after he saw my CT scan. My appendix had burst, but the infection encapsulated itself into a sealed pocket around my appendix. It had not spread all over the inside of my body, which would likely have killed me. I spent four days in the hospital corralling the infection, then a month and a half resting and healing at home.

"We have something to show you," Randy says as he walks Luna out of her corral and over to the round pen. Her muscles are tight and lean. The lower edge of her ribcage is showing through her thin summer coat.

"We've been working with her every chance we get. Tuesdays and Thursdays, plus Sundays after brunch." Tony carries the saddle and blanket over to the round pen and throws it atop the rail. "You just sit here. We're gonna show you how she's doing."

Eliza and Olivia come over and hand me a bottled water. They stand by my side, each one with a hand on my shoulder.

"We are so glad you are feeling better, Ginger," Eliza smiles and tells me. "These guys are so excited to show you what they've been doing with Luna."

Joey comes out of the tack room with a bridle and hangs it on the gate. He climbs over the top rail, looks back at me and waves, then heads over to Luna. Luna adores Joey. She will do just about anything he asks. Randy lays the blue tarp on the ground inside the pen and spreads it out wide. Joey and Luna walk back and forth across the tarp as it crackles under their feet. Without a halter or lead over her neck, Luna follows Joey over the blue plastic, occasionally stretching her neck down to take in a sniff. After a few minutes Joey picks up the tarp, spreads it over the full length of Luna's body and starts walking the perimeter of the round pen.

Luna carries her head low and blows out gently from her nostrils. The tarp swings along as they go. It is a long, blue dress that drags the ground on either side of her body. She shows no concern. Her eyes are as soft as cotton balls; she blinks them shut, then open, every few minutes without a care.

Fear was the lens from which Luna always saw the world. She was hardwired for surprise. Her entire body was spring-loaded to obey her eyes' command. The shape of her eyes always told her story. Looking at her now, she doesn't even slightly resemble the animal I once knew.

"Change can be immediate," one of my teachers told me a long time ago. Once a horse makes a change, you won't be obliged to go back every day and repeat yourself. They will remember it. Even if they don't see you for another ten years, once you return, they will remember you.

For the last year, I have seen a version of myself in Luna. Her isolation, her inability to trust anyone, her not being able to be at home in this community; Luna has, on many occasions, reminded me of my own lonely, reclusive childhood. Now I watch her doze around the round pen, looking more like a stuffed animal than the fierce beast she once emulated. Sitting atop Randy's mounting box, I watch Luna and Joey sway along, like two old friends out for a walk. I wonder, have I changed, like Luna, into a softer creature? One who can finally trust others and feel like she belongs?

Randy enters through the gate. Luna stops alongside Joey, who slides the tarp off her back and throws it over the rail. Still without a lead rope or halter on, Luna stands next to Joey and doesn't take a step. Randy throws the saddle blanket over her back. Adjusts it up to her withers and makes sure it sits just right on her back. She doesn't move. He brings the saddle over, flips it onto her back, and takes his time cinching it down tight. Luna yawns.

We have tried to place a saddle on Luna's back before but have never succeeded. She would twirl and spin around us when we got close, kicking out sideways to defend herself from the foreign object.

Eliza squeezes my shoulder from above. "You have given us all this, Ginger." I look up and see her thoughtfully watching Randy's every move. "We are horsemen now. Real horsemen." I reach up and squeeze her hand. If I look into her eyes, I know I'll lose it.

One of these days, sometime in the future, Tony, Eliza, and Randy will leave this ranch. As soon as their prison term is up, they will reenter our world. Joey and Olivia will eventually move on, too. I'll be left here, with Luna and her herd. Maybe more residents will join livestock, maybe many more. I must let my fear, my loneliness, my desire to cut and run—I must let it go. Change can be immediate.

"We are saving lives," I heard Eliza say a few months ago, to a woman who was interviewing to come onto the ranch from prison. "One life at a time."

"We aren't done yet." Tony walks up from behind me. He picks the bridle off the gate and climbs over the top rail. "Oh no. There's more." He is so light on his feet that I think he's going to blow away in the breeze.

Tony spreads the bit between his thumb and pinky, then tickles Luna's lips with his opposite thumb. She parts her lips and the bit and bridle slide into her mouth and over her ears. We have never had a bridle on Luna. She chews lightly on the taste of the metal lying over her tongue. Tony gets along her left side and bends her neck gently. Her neck curves around, loose like a rubber band. He begins to twist the stirrup around, ready to place his left boot in its center.

"Whoa. Wait a minute." Surprised, I stand and walk up to the rail. Everyone gathers closer to me, reaching for me, making sure I don't fall.

I hesitate. I think I'm going to say, "No, Tony. Let's wait." But it doesn't come out of my mouth. Tony has his boot in the stirrup, bouncing up toward the saddle, then back to the ground. Luna has one ear flipped onto Tony, showing a quiet interest. Her eyes still kind and gentle.

"Where is the blue rider's helmet I brought over?" I ask everyone. Eliza runs off to the tack room and brings it back. "Put this on, Tony," I tell him. "And, Randy, slide a halter and lead on her, too, please." Randy hustles to get a halter, then slides it under the bridle.

Tony has both feet back on the ground. He turns and faces me, waiting for my approval.

"Can I swing up?" Tony asks me.

"If you think she's ready." But in my heart, I know she is.

ACKNOWLEDGMENTS

These essays have appeared in modified form in other publications as follows:

"Learning to Walk," in *Witness* magazine, Spring 2016, edited by Maile Chapman. *Utne Reader* republished this chapter in Fall 2016, edited by Christian Williams.

"Broken," in *Animal* magazine, July 2016, edited by Danita Berg.

"Centaur," in *Quarterly West*, no. 91, June 27, 2017.

"Moon and Star," in *Tin House* magazine, Winter 2017, edited by Emma Komlos-Hrobsky.

Gratitude

For many years, horse owners have trusted me to ride, train, and help their horses. The intimacy of listening to and learning from these horses over a long period of time gave me the gift of language and sight. It is these horses, and their owners, that made the writing of this book possible. And to my horses—especially Belle, Moo, and Izzy—who save me.

I started writing this book while getting my MFA in creative writing at the Institute of American Indian Arts in New Mexico. The community of faculty and students in this program created one of the most inspiring moments of my life. I thank Chip Livingston, Ina Lenard, Kat Wilder, and everyone in the poetry department who set the standard for raw, beautiful, and vulnerable writing. Pam Houston inspired me endlessly in the grounding details of my physical experience. Melissa Febos and Lidia Yuknavitch gave me the courage to write the hard stuff.

For two years I worked with the writer Jamie Figueroa, who slowly walked me through these pages with such care and delicacy, coaching me about the craft and the art of writing. And my dear friend Heather Laab helped me edit the first versions of these stories before I submitted them for publication.

Corporeal Writing, Tin House, Writing X Writers, and Writers at Work offered me fellowships and residencies, which gave me the confidence to keep pushing these stories forward.

My partner Glenda Fletcher has been my go-to reader for each and every chapter. My first reader, my last reader. A songwriter by trade, her ability to find the heart in every story and polish it has helped keep this book on its emotional path.

Throughout the writing of this book I have been blessed with the strength, support, and love from the amazing women in my family. Judy Primoli, Lynn Meighan, Trish Kridler, Kathleen Homo, and Carol Gaffney; their presence sits between the pages of this book.

Thank you, Elizabeth Wales, my agent, who exemplifies that book publishing is still a very beautiful human endeavor. And to Tom Mayer, my editor, who guided me gently into making this book better and better. I know how fortunate I am to have you both in my corner.

I don't know how to thank all the amazing men and women in recovery, and out of prison, whom I have met over the last seven years. You have changed my life forever. I hope I have helped support you as much as I have been inspired by the life you continue to fight toward. I have tried to capture a sliver of truth here in these pages so that perhaps the readers of this book can start to admire the person behind the addiction as much as I have. To all of you. This book is dedicated to you.

HALF BROKE

Ginger Gaffney

HALF BROKE

Ginger Gaffney

DISCUSSION QUESTIONS

1. What does the title of this memoir, *Half Broke*, mean to you?

2. Gaffney writes that horses "blend themselves to the inside of a person: emotional camouflage" (p. 8). What does "emotional camouflage" look like on the ranch? What do the horses seem to need emotionally from the residents? What do they get instead?

3. "Flight, not fight," Gaffney writes, "is how horses naturally resolve troubling situations" (p. 9). Why do the horses on the ranch choose to fight? How does their behavior reflect the mood and organization of the ranch?

4. Describe Gaffney and the residents at the beginning of *Half Broke*. How willing are they to trust each other? How does Gaffney earn the residents' trust? How does trust shape their relationship?

5. Gaffney writes about her childhood struggle with extreme shyness. "Unable to speak," she writes, "I learned to watch bodies" (p. 38). How does Gaffney's acute sensitivity to body language serve her?

6. When Gaffney first encounters Belle, "the intimacy of it fills [her] with the same fear [she has] had with lovers" (p. 45). What do you think Gaffney means here? Were you able to identify with this feeling? How?

7. Gaffney didn't come out to her mother as a lesbian; her mother discovered Carla's letters in a dresser drawer. "I

didn't speak to my mother about those letters for eight years," Gaffney writes. "I learned to hide, to become invisible again. I learned to lie" (p. 61). Why do you think Gaffney chose to hide and lie about her sexuality? Was this an act of protection? Self-preservation? Do you think Gaffney's formative experiences as a lesbian make her especially suited to working with abused horses and people? Why or why not?

8. Gaffney worries about what to do with the residents' "broken parts: their lack of attention span, their wounded bodies, their anger, the dullness in their eyes" (p. 63). Why do you think she is so attuned to their brokenness? How does she relate? And how does empathy inform the training she offers?

9. Gaffney tells the residents, "How you walk, how you hold your posture, this will tell horses whether to stomp you or follow you. It also tells them whether you are trustworthy or a fake" (p. 65). What do you think "fake" means here? Have you witnessed this dynamic before in your life? When?

10. Randy mutters "fuck this" when he struggles to untie Billy (p. 68). His "arrogance and fake bravado" also offend other residents (p. 109). Did you feel for Randy in the beginning? Did your opinion of him change? What about the other residents? Did you feel differently about them as you saw them transform through their work with the horses? Who changes the most?

11. Gaffney confesses to the reader that the ranch "feels like home" (p. 101). What do you think "home" means to Gaffney? Did you worry about how attached Gaffney becomes to the residents and their horses? Why or why not?

12. "The rules on the ranch are clear," Gaffney writes. "Don't dwell on who you were before. Be the person you are becoming" (p. 116). Why do you think these rules appeal

to Gaffney? Do these rules seem particularly helpful for survivors of trauma? Why or why not?

13. Sarah says, "You know, Ginger, I'm more than half-broke. I need these walls. These fences" (p. 138). Do you agree with Sarah? Does she need to be on the ranch? How does her life on the ranch compare with her life before prison? Why might she feel afraid to leave the ranch?

14. When Gaffney discovers a box containing drugs and condoms in the hay barn, she knows she has to report it. Were you surprised by Gaffney's discovery and how she handles it? Did you have any idea who the box might belong to? How does Gaffney's perception of herself and her role on the ranch change after this incident?

15. It turns out that Sarah is at least partly responsible for the box. Did you feel sympathy for her? Why or why not? Gaffney wonders if Sarah will "tell everything" to James and Marcos and "keep her place on the ranch secure" (p. 149). What would you have done in Sarah's shoes?

16. Gaffney writes, "The mistake I made, my ultimate failure, was to think what I had with the livestock team was permanent. That nothing could touch it. I should have known better" (p. 154). Do you think Gaffney was naive? Is she fair to herself when she calls what happened *her* failure?

17. Sarah, Flor, Omar, and Paul are dropped in a Walmart parking lot after one phone call. Were you surprised by this? Did other rules and procedures on the ranch strike you as unfair or inhumane? Did you ever feel as if these rules and procedures impeded residents' recovery? Why or why not?

18. After a year on the ranch, Gaffney wonders if she, like

Luna, has become a "softer creature" (p. 242). Do you think she is "softer" as a result of her experience with the residents and their horses? If so, how does she demonstrate softness? How has her outlook on life changed?

For a complete list of Norton's works with reading group guides, please go to wwnorton.com/reading-guides.

Diana Abu-Jaber	*Life Without a Recipe*
Diane Ackerman	*The Zookeeper's Wife*
Michelle Adelman	*Piece of Mind*
Molly Antopol	*The UnAmericans*
Andrea Barrett	*Archangel*
Rowan Hisayo Buchanan	*Harmless Like You*
Ada Calhoun	*Wedding Toasts I'll Never Give*
Bonnie Jo Campbell	*Mothers, Tell Your Daughters*
	Once Upon a River
Lan Samantha Chang	*Inheritance*
Ann Cherian	*A Good Indian Wife*
Evgenia Citkowitz	*The Shades*
Amanda Coe	*The Love She Left Behind*
Michael Cox	*The Meaning of Night*
Jeremy Dauber	*Jewish Comedy*
Jared Diamond	*Guns, Germs, and Steel*
Caitlin Doughty	*From Here to Eternity*
Andre Dubus III	*House of Sand and Fog*
	Townie: A Memoir
Anne Enright	*The Forgotten Waltz*
	The Green Road
Amanda Filipacchi	*The Unfortunate Importance of Beauty*
Beth Ann Fennelly	*Heating & Cooling*
Betty Friedan	*The Feminine Mystique*
Maureen Gibbon	*Paris Red*
Stephen Greenblatt	*The Swerve*
Lawrence Hill	*The Illegal*
	Someone Knows My Name
Ann Hood	*The Book That Matters Most*
	The Obituary Writer
Dara Horn	*A Guide for the Perplexed*
Blair Hurley	*The Devoted*

Meghan Kenny	*The Driest Season*
Nicole Krauss	*The History of Love*
Don Lee	*The Collective*
Amy Liptrot	*The Outrun: A Memoir*
Donna M. Lucey	*Sargent's Women*
Bernard MacLaverty	*Midwinter Break*
Maaza Mengiste	*Beneath the Lion's Gaze*
Claire Messud	*The Burning Girl*
	When the World Was Steady
Liz Moore	*Heft*
	The Unseen World
Neel Mukherjee	*The Lives of Others*
	A State of Freedom
Janice P. Nimura	*Daughters of the Samurai*
Rachel Pearson	*No Apparent Distress*
Richard Powers	*Orfeo*
Kirstin Valdez Quade	*Night at the Fiestas*
Jean Rhys	*Wide Sargasso Sea*
Mary Roach	*Packing for Mars*
Somini Sengupta	*The End of Karma*
Akhil Sharma	*Family Life*
	A Life of Adventure and Delight
Joan Silber	*Fools*
Johanna Skibsrud	*Quartet for the End of Time*
Mark Slouka	*Brewster*
Kate Southwood	*Evensong*
Manil Suri	*The City of Devi*
	The Age of Shiva
Madeleine Thien	*Do Not Say We Have Nothing*
	Dogs at the Perimeter
Vu Tran	*Dragonfish*
Rose Tremain	*The American Lover*
	The Gustav Sonata
Brady Udall	*The Lonely Polygamist*
Brad Watson	*Miss Jane*
Constance Fenimore Woolson	*Miss Grief and Other Stories*